Cooking Class

Global Feast!

44 RECIPES
That Celebrate the
World's Cultures

Deanna F. Cook

Storey Publishing

This book is dedicated to Doug, who
traveled the world with me on a food adventure
to collect recipes from kids many moons ago.

Acknowledgments

Many thanks to the great kids who cooked with me in my kitchen and appeared in all the wonderful photos throughout this book: Amelia, Bodhi, Coco, Dhyuthi, Ella, Inez, Jayden, Jovan, Kobi, Leila, Leo, Lily, Liv, Lukas, Maceo, Maisie, Malia, Margaret, Matthew, Mekdes, Olive, Pranav, Salim, Song, Tao, Tejas, Viva, Wolf, Xavier, Zadie H., Zadie S., and Zora.

Special thanks to Carl Tremblay and his assistant, Kam Mitchell, for the beautiful photos, and to talented food stylist Joy Howard. Special thanks to Jessica Armstrong, Michal Lumsden, Deborah Balmuth, and the whole team at Storey who helped make this book the best it could be.

Thanks to the children I met on my world travels as a Watson Fellow in 1989 who inspired some of the recipes in this book and appeared in my first book, *The Kids' Multicultural Cookbook*.

I could not have made this book without the support of my family, who tested and tasted many of the recipes. Thanks, Ella, Maisie, and Doug!

To all the readers of this book: Thanks for picking up *Cooking Class Global Feast!* I hope you enjoy learning about the world by making the recipes in this book. Please share photos of your recipes with me at DeannaFCook.com — I'd love to see what you cook up!

CONTENTS

Welcome to the
GLOBAL KITCHEN

Get ready to travel the world without ever leaving your home!

The recipes in this book are inspired by the amazing flavors all around the world. If you want to get a taste for how kids with backgrounds different from yours eat, head to the kitchen and stir up some international favorites from the following pages!

Cooking foods from around the world is a great way to learn about different cultures and people. Look closely at the ingredients list for each recipe and you'll discover what foods are available in each country. Follow the recipe directions and you'll learn a little about cooking techniques across the globe. Serve yourself an international meal and brush up on that country's food traditions and eating customs.

When you're ready to get cooking, flip through this book and pick a recipe that looks tasty to you. Choose a recipe from a country you've always wanted to visit. Or try one from your own heritage. My own kids are part Lebanese and part Scottish, and they love making Mujadara (page 108) and Sweet Shortbread (page 126). Whatever recipe you pick, you'll have fun in the kitchen and learn worlds about cooking global foods.

Read the Real Kids Cook sidebars to meet some of the kids who are pictured in this book. You'll get to know a bit of each kid's family heritage, plus the names of the recipes they love to make. They may inspire you to try a recipe.

Happy cooking!

Deanna F. Cook

WHERE IN THE WORLD?

HELLO!

Hola!

Marhaba

KONNICHIWA

NAMASTE

Ni Hǎo

SHALOM

Chapter 1
≫ HELLO! ≪

Put on your apron and follow these tips for international cooking fun!

RECIPE RATINGS

Each recipe is rated with one, two, or three spoons so you know the skill level needed to complete it. If you are a new chef, you can start with the easier recipes and work your way up.

1 SPOON: Most of these recipes do not involve baking or cooking and can be pulled together without having to use the stovetop or oven.

2 SPOONS: These recipes involve cooking over the stovetop or baking in the oven. Brush up on your stovetop and oven safety skills before you begin (see page 18).

3 SPOONS: These are good recipes to work on with a parent or older sibling. The recipes involve cutting with sharp knives, using an electric mixer or food processor, and using the oven. They tend to take more time to prepare, too.

Lesson 1
READ UP ON KITCHEN RULES

When you're ready to start cooking, follow these basic kitchen rules. Be sure to ask for help, if you need it, in your cooking adventures.

1 **Start by asking an adult for permission.** Have a grown-up cook with you if you are working over the hot stove, baking in the oven, or using a sharp knife.

2 **Wash your hands** with warm water and soap before you handle food.

3 **Roll up long sleeves and wear an apron.** Tie back long hair to keep it away from food. Stand on a stool if you can't reach the counter or stove.

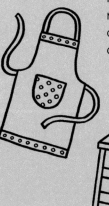

4 **Read the recipe from start to finish** before you begin. Follow the recipe steps closely.

5 **Put out all the ingredients you'll need** (see the recipe's "Here's What You Need" list) to be sure you have everything. If you are missing something, make a list and have a grown-up take you to the grocery store *before* you start your cooking project.

6 **Wash all the fruits and vegetables you'll need** before you start chopping and measuring.

7 **Take out all the tools you'll need** for your recipe, from measuring cups to bowls.

8 **Measure carefully** (see the tips on page 22).

9 **Preheat.** Let the oven come to the correct temperature before you put in your pans or baking sheets. If you don't preheat the oven, your food will take longer to bake or will cook unevenly.

10 **Use a timer.** But if the dish doesn't seem quite done when the timer goes off, let it cook for another 5 minutes or so.

11 **Stay in the kitchen!** Never leave the room if you are cooking something on the stove or baking in the oven.

12 **Always use pot holders** when moving pans in and out of the oven or touching hot handles on the stovetop.

13 **Trust your sense of smell.** If you smell something burning, move the food off the hot stove and lower the heat (or turn it off altogether). If you're baking and smell food burning, turn the oven off and take the food out, even if the timer hasn't gone off yet.

14 **Give your food a taste test.** If you'd like it to be more flavorful, add a little salt (which helps bring out flavor). Or add extra spice. Part of the fun and creativity in cooking is customizing flavors to match your personal tastes.

15 **Remember to turn the stove or oven off** after you're done cooking.

16 **Leave the kitchen sparkling clean!** Put away the ingredients, wipe down the countertop, and wash the dishes.

Lesson 2
GATHER THE RIGHT TOOLS

To make the recipes in this book, you'll need some basic pots and pans. You'll also need baking tools, such as baking sheets, measuring cups, mixing spoons, and pot holders. Some recipes require global cooking tools, such as a bamboo steamer or a wok. If you don't have them, buy them or borrow them from a friend or neighbor.

WHISK

MIXING BOWLS

SPATULA

FOOD PROCESSOR

Chop

DRY MEASURING CUPS

CUTTING

BOARDS

LIQUID MEASURING CUPS

RAMEKINS

GARLIC PRESS

KNIVES

KITCHEN SCISSORS

GRATER

CUPCAKE TIN & LINERS

SKILLET

BAKING SHEET

PARCHMENT PAPER

WOODEN SPOON

POT HOLDER

SOUP POT

TONGS

WOODEN SKEWERS

RUBBER SPATULA

PIZZA WHEEL

WOK

PASTRY BRUSH

BAMBOO STEAMER

13

Lesson 3
STOCK UP ON GLOBAL INGREDIENTS

Look through the recipes in the book, then make a list of the ingredients you need to make a few dishes. If you plan to cook international foods often, it's a good idea to stock up on some of the basics shown here. With the right ingredients in your cupboard, you'll have everything you need to whip up a global dinner or treat anytime!

YOGURT

BUTTER

SALT

PEPPER

VANILLA EXTRACT

SUGAR

EGGS

MILK

CORNMEAL

CINNAMON

COCOA POWDER

WHITE FLOUR

BAKING POWDER
and baking soda

COCONUT

SESAME SEEDS

SEEDS, NUTS & DRIED FRUIT

GOLDEN SYRUP

FLOURS

WHOLE-WHEAT FLOUR

PEANUTS

RAISINS

BLACK BEANS

NOODLES

OILS

RAMEN

BASMATI RICE

BROWN RICE

DRIED GRAINS

BEANS

GINGER

SPICES

LENTILS

HERBS

FRESH VEGETABLES

SOY SAUCE

Lesson 4
DO YOUR KITCHEN PREP WORK

Many of the recipes in this book call for some prep work, such as grating carrots or crushing garlic, before you actually make the dish. Read the ingredients list to find out what you need to do. With all your prep work done in advance, you won't have to stop what you're doing as you cook. Here are some kitchen skills you'll need to use in the recipes.

Chop and dice: to cut vegetables and other foods into small pieces with a sharp knife (and a grown-up's help). To **chop**, cut food into pieces about 1 inch square. To **dice**, cut it about ½ inch square.

Mince: to cut herbs and other foods into tiny pieces using a small knife or clean kitchen scissors.

Juice: to squeeze the juice from a lime or lemon by cutting it in half and then pressing the halves on a juicer. Twist the fruit back and forth to get out all the juice.

Crush garlic: to mash raw garlic. You'll need a garlic press. Peel off the papery skin of one clove. Put it into the press and squeeze the press shut. The crushed garlic will ooze out of the end.

Grate: to rub cheese, a carrot, ginger, or another food against a grater to shred it. If the piece of food you're holding gets too small, stop grating to protect your fingers.

Peel: to remove the skin from a fruit or vegetable by peeling it with a vegetable peeler. There are two kinds of peelers: straight peelers (shown) and Y-shaped peelers.

How to...

WASH LETTUCE & FRESH HERBS

1 Fill a salad spinner with cold water and add the lettuce leaves or fresh herbs. Let sit for 5 minutes or more. The dirt will sink to the bottom.

2 Lift the spinner basket out of the water. Drain the water. Put the basket of lettuce or herbs back in the empty spinner.

3 Put on the cover. Press the top and start spinning. The water will fling out, leaving the lettuce or herbs dry.

CHOP AN ONION

1 Cut the onion in half lengthwise. Lay the halves flat on a cutting board and cut off the ends. Peel off the skin.

2 Slice one onion in half crosswise. Make as many cut lines as you can fit on the onion. Hold the knife firmly and tuck your fingers back.

3 Flip the onion slices sideways and lay them flat on the cutting board. Cut downward to dice. Then, finish off with a quick chop. Repeat steps 2 and 3 with the other half.

Lesson 5
SHARPEN YOUR STOVETOP SKILLS

Read the recipe's "Here's What You Do" directions carefully. You'll notice some of the following key kitchen terms in those directions. Refer to these skills if you're not sure what to do in the directions.

Stir: to mix ingredients with a spoon, whisk, or spatula. Don't use metal spoons or spatulas with nonstick pans.

Whisk: to combine ingredients with a whisk. You can whisk eggs and milk in a bowl or whisk sauces over the stovetop.

Fry: to cook food in an open pan in hot oil. Frying food can splatter the hot oil, so watch out.

Grill: to cook food over a gas or charcoal fire outside.

Melt: to turn a solid into a liquid by applying heat. You can melt butter in a saucepan or skillet over low heat or in a bowl in a microwave. You can melt cheese in the oven.

Sauté: to cook food lightly in a little oil in a skillet.

Simmer: to cook liquid slowly over low heat. The bubbles rise to the surface much more slowly when simmering than they do when boiling.

Toast: to brown lightly on both sides. You can do this on a griddle or in a toaster, an oven, or a toaster oven.

Boil: to heat liquid to a temperature high enough that bubbles form and break rapidly on the surface. When boiling, always use a saucepan that is big enough to keep ingredients from boiling over the top.

Steam: to cook food in a bamboo or metal basket placed over simmering water. The water vaporizes and makes steam, which heats and cooks the food.

How to...
GRATE FRESH GINGER

Many Asian dishes, such as fried rice (page 104), are flavored with fresh ginger.

1 Peel the ginger with a vegetable peeler.

2 Rub the ginger against the side of a cheese grater. To dice it, chop it into small cubes with a paring knife.

19

Lesson 6
BRUSH UP ON BAKING TERMS

If you are baking some of the cookies or breads in this book, you may need to remind yourself about these essential skills before you put your food in the oven.

Mix: to use a spoon or electric mixer to combine ingredients evenly. Use a bowl that is big enough to hold everything with extra room for the mixing activity.

Cream: for this book, *creaming* means mixing butter and sugar together with an electric mixer until the combination turns fluffy. This adds air to your mixture, which helps your baked goods rise.

Beat: to mix rapidly with a wooden spoon, wire whisk, or electric mixer until smooth.

Grease the pan: to rub vegetable oil or butter (or use baking spray) on baking pans so food won't stick. Don't forget to grease the sides and corners of the pan!

Line with parchment: to lay a sheet of parchment paper on your pan, which will keep cookies and breads from sticking to the bottom.

Knead: to fold dough over, press with your palms, then turn and fold again. This develops gluten, which makes bread light and airy.

Brush: to paint vegetable oil or egg wash on dough or bread with a pastry brush.

Add dry ingredients: to add a mixture of flour and other dry ingredients to a batter. If you're using a stand mixer, you can prevent the flour from flying around the kitchen by carefully holding a dish towel around the bowl, keeping your fingers out of the way.

Cut in the butter: to use a special pastry cutter, or two forks, to combine butter or shortening with dry ingredients until crumbly.

Scrape with a spatula: to get every last bit of batter out of a bowl or off your equipment with a rubber spatula.

Cut with a pizza wheel: to slice food into pieces using a wheel. Simply hold the pizza wheel firmly and roll it through the food in a straight line moving away from your body.

Test for doneness: to check that your baked goods are finished baking. Insert a toothpick into the center. If it comes out clean and dry, the baked goods are done.

Equivalents & Conversions

Here's a handy chart to help you convert recipe measurements.

1 TEASPOON
= 5 milliliters

1 TABLESPOON
= 3 teaspoons
(or ½ fluid ounce)
= 15 milliliters

¼ CUP
= 4 tablespoons
= 60 milliliters

½ CUP
= 4 ounces
= 120 milliliters

1 CUP
= 8 ounces
= 240 milliliters

1 PINT
= 2 cups
= 16 ounces
= 475 milliliters

1 QUART
= 2 pints
= 0.95 liter

Lesson 7
MEASURE CAREFULLY

When following a recipe, it's important to measure the ingredients carefully. Here are some tips.

Butter. Follow the measurement marks on the butter package. Find the line for the correct amount, then carefully cut straight down on the stick through the paper. Unwrap the portion you need and add it to your recipe.

Dry ingredients. Measure flour, sugar, and other dry ingredients with dry measuring cups or measuring spoons that can be leveled off. Fill the cup or spoon with the ingredient, then run the flat part of a butter knife across it to get an exact measurement.

Liquid ingredients. Measure larger amounts of milk, water, coconut milk, vegetable oil, and other liquids in a glass or plastic liquid measuring cup. Pour the liquid into the cup and read the measurement from the side.

For smaller amounts, like teaspoons, use measuring spoons. Work over a small bowl to catch any spills.

Lesson 8
PRACTICE KITCHEN SAFETY

Many of the recipes in this book require that you keep safety measures in mind, especially when you use sharp knives, an electric mixer, or a hot stovetop or oven. It's important to work safely in the kitchen, so here are some tips.

Knife and grater. Make sure your knife is sharpened properly (dull knives are more dangerous because they can slip while you're cutting), and hold it firmly, with your fingers out of the way of the blade. Always cut with the blade moving away from your hand.

When you use a grater, watch out that you don't accidentally scrape your fingertips or your knuckles. Dry your hands when cutting and grating — wet hands are slippery!

Mixer, food processor, and blender. Always keep the cord tucked back so it isn't in your way. Unplug the appliance when you are done. Keep your fingers out of the way of the beaters when working with an electric mixer. Use the lock setting on a stand mixer to keep the bowl and beater in place while you mix.

With a food processor, be especially careful when you are fitting the blades into the machine or taking them out to be washed. Read the manual or ask an adult for help the first time. Never try to operate a food processor with the lid off.

When using a blender, be sure the lid is on tight before you blend, and *never* touch the sharp blades.

Microwave. Different microwave ovens have different directions, so ask an adult to show you how to use yours. Never use metal or aluminum foil in the microwave. Always use microwave-safe dishes. Glass, paper towels, and some plastic containers are fine. The wrong material could damage the microwave or even cause a fire.

Stovetop. Before you turn on the stove, check first with an adult. He or she can show you the proper way to use the range and explain the different settings. Turn pan handles to the side so the pans don't accidentally get knocked off the stove. Be extra careful of hot liquids splattering (they can cause serious burns). Switch off the stovetop when you have finished cooking. And remember: pots can stay hot even after they're taken off the stove.

Oven. Keep the oven closed while the food is baking for the best (and safest) results. When you do open the oven, avoid the blast of heat that will rise up in your face. Always use oven mitts when handling hot baking trays.

Lesson 9
CELEBRATE WORLD FLAVORS

There are lots of ways to have fun with foods from different countries. Here are just a few.

Taste new foods at restaurants. Want to learn more about international foods? Go out to eat at a restaurant in your hometown or in a city you're visiting. See how many different foods you can taste at Chinese, Japanese, Indian, Italian, Ethiopian, or other global restaurants. When you get home, try making one of the recipes in your own kitchen.

Shop at international stores. Looking for a spicy curry powder or sweet rice for a recipe? Take a trip to the grocery store and look at the international section. If you don't find what you're looking for, visit an international grocery store in your area.

Buy some global breads, candies, or fruit and give them a taste test. For ideas, see the Global Taste Test sections throughout the book.

Host a global dinner party. Pick a country and make foods from that place with your family or friends. Research the country's food traditions and eating customs. Add special touches to your dinner party, from global music to traditional clothing. You may even use napkins or a tablecloth featuring textile designs from that country.

How to Use Chopsticks

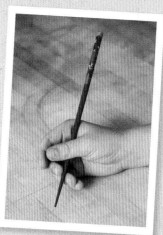

1 In your dominant hand, hold one chopstick in the crook of the thumb with it resting on the third finger.

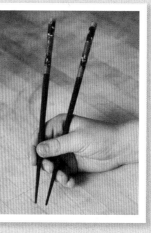

2 Add the upper chopstick, holding it between the tip of the thumb and the first two fingers.

3 Pick up your food by using your index (or first) finger to lower and raise the top chopstick, keeping the lower chopstick stable (not moving).

Host a multicultural night. Looking for a fun way to celebrate the diversity of all the kids in your school or community center? Host an international night. You and your friends can each prepare a table to showcase one of the ethnicities from your background. Include maps, fun facts, props (such as local currency or clothing), and of course food for everyone to sample.

Spin the globe. If you're stumped on what to cook for dinner, spin a globe, close your eyes, and point. Try cooking a recipe from wherever your finger lands!

SAWUBONA

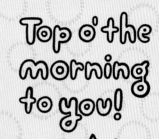
Top o' the morning to you!

BONJOUR

Selamat pagi

GUTEN MORGEN

KASHA, page 36

Chapter 2
BREAKFAST

Start your day with flavors of some of the world's favorite breakfasts, from Belgian waffles to Irish soda bread to Russian porridge.

CANADA
Fried Bannock Bread, 28

GERMANY
Apfelpfannkuchen, 30

ENGLAND
Beans on Toast, 32

IRELAND
Soda Bread, 34

RUSSIA
Kasha, 36

SOUTH AFRICA
Mealie Meal Bread, 40

BELGIUM
Wonderful Waffles, 42

TONGA
Coconut Bread, 44

GLOBAL TASTE TEST:
Fruits, 38

FRIED BANNOCK BREAD 🥄🥄

Makes 12 pieces

Versions of this easy-to-make quick bread are a staple in native communities throughout Canada. You can bake it in the oven, cook it over the campfire, or even fry it up in a pan like we do here. However you make it, bannock tastes yummy with a little butter and jam or Canadian maple syrup!

Here's What You Need

- 3 cups flour
- 2 tablespoons baking powder
- 1½ teaspoons salt
- 1½ cups warm water
- Maple syrup (optional)

HERE'S WHAT YOU DO

1. Whisk together the flour, baking powder, and salt in large bowl. Add the warm water.

2. Stir until the dough comes together in a ball.

3.

Turn the sticky dough out onto a floured countertop. Sprinkle with extra flour if it's too sticky to handle.

4.

Pat the dough into a big oval shape.

5.

Use a pizza wheel to divide the dough into a dozen fist-size pieces.

6.

Heat ¼ inch of vegetable oil in a large skillet over medium-high heat. When the oil is hot, carefully fry the bannock on both sides until it's golden brown. Serve with maple syrup for dipping, if you like!

GET CREATIVE

Baked Bannock

Preheat the oven to 400°F (200°C). Follow the recipe through step 4, shaping the dough into a big oval. Place the dough on a baking sheet lined with parchment paper or greased with vegetable oil. Bake for about 30 minutes, until the bread turns golden brown. Slice and serve warm or cooled.

GERMANY

APFELPFANNKUCHEN

Makes about 3 large pancakes

In Germany, kids love to make these big, thick pancakes filled with apples. Instead of topping pancakes with maple syrup, German kids use whipped cream or a little applesauce and cinnamon sugar.

Here's What You Need

- 1 cup flour
- 1 teaspoon baking powder
- ½ teaspoon baking soda
- 1 teaspoon ground cinnamon
- ¼ teaspoon salt
- 2 eggs
- 1 cup milk

- 2 tablespoons vegetable oil
- Butter
- 2 apples, peeled, cored, and thinly sliced

OPTIONAL TOPPINGS:

Whipped cream or applesauce
Cinnamon sugar

SAY WHAT?!

In German, *apfel* means "apple" and *pfannkuchen* means "pancake." Put them together and you get **Apfelpfannkuchen** (ap-ful-FAN-koo-kuhn).

1.

Whisk together the flour, baking powder, baking soda, cinnamon, and salt in a large mixing bowl.

2.

Beat the eggs in a medium bowl. Add the milk and oil, and mix well. Pour the egg mixture over the flour mixture and stir until smooth.

3.

Melt a pat of butter in a large skillet over medium heat. Arrange some of the apple slices toward the center of the skillet and let them cook for about a minute.

4.

Pour enough batter into the skillet to cover the apples.

5.

When bubbles begin to appear on the surface of the pancake, lift it with a spatula and peek underneath. If it looks light brown, flip it over. When the other side looks tan, remove the pancake from the skillet.

6.

Transfer the finished pancake to a plate. Top with whipped cream or applesauce and/or cinnamon sugar, if you'd like. Repeat steps 3 through 5 until all the apples and batter are used up.

ENGLAND

BEANS ON TOAST

Makes 1 serving

Some kids in England like to make toast and top it with canned beans! You can find beans in tomato sauce in the canned vegetable section of most grocery stores, but you'll need to look closely.

Here's What You Need

1 slice bread
2 tablespoons canned British beans in tomato sauce
2 tablespoons grated cheese

HERE'S WHAT YOU DO

1.
Toast the bread until golden brown.

2.
Place the toasted bread on a toaster-oven tray. Spoon your beans onto the toast.

3.
Sprinkle on the cheese. Melt the cheese by broiling in the toaster oven for 1 minute. Eat right away!

GET CREATIVE
British Breakfast

For a classic English breakfast, try this:

1 fried egg

1 piece toast

Breakfast sausage (known as "bangers" in England)

Fried tomato

English breakfast tea with milk and sugar

¼ cup canned beans in tomato sauce, heated up

REAL KIDS COOK
Meet Wolf (9) and Viva (11)

FAMILY HERITAGE:
England and Scotland

RECIPES WE'VE MADE:
Yorkshire pudding, gravy, beans on toast, baked mac & cheese, and cake

FAVORITE INTERNATIONAL FOODS:
Mexican

"Sometimes we go to England to visit our Nana, who lives there."

REAL KIDS COOK

Meet Lukas (2), Jovan (11), and Tejas (8)

FAMILY HERITAGE:
Germany, Ireland, Norway, Poland, and Sweden

RECIPES WE'VE MADE:
Irish soda bread, quesadillas, and popcorn

FAVORITE INTERNATIONAL FOODS:
Mexican and Indian

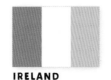

IRELAND

SODA BREAD

Makes 1 loaf

This traditional Irish bread rises in the oven with the help of baking soda (not yeast!). Slice and serve warm with Irish butter and jam.

Here's What You Need

- 2 cups flour
- 2 cups whole-wheat flour (or 2 more cups white flour)
- ¼ cup sugar
- 2 teaspoons baking soda
- 1 tablespoon baking powder
- 1 teaspoon salt
- 4 tablespoons butter, cut into small pieces
- 2 cups buttermilk
- 1 cup currants or raisins (optional)

Preheat the oven to 375°F (190°C).

1. Stir the flours, sugar, baking soda, baking powder, and salt in a large bowl.

2. Mix the butter into the dry ingredients using a pastry cutter or fork. The dough should become crumbly.

3. Pour in the buttermilk and currants, if using, and stir until the dough forms a rough ball. You can switch to mixing with your (clean!) hands if it's too hard to stir. The dough will be a little bit sticky, so dip your hands in flour first.

4. Transfer the dough to a countertop dusted with flour. Knead the dough for a minute or two, then pat it into a big ball.

5. Line a baking sheet with parchment paper (or grease it with vegetable oil). Place the dough on the baking sheet and cut a big X in the top.

6. Bake for 40 to 50 minutes, or until the crust is golden brown.

KASHA

Makes 4 servings

This creamy porridge is a staple breakfast food in Russia. It's warm, sweet, buttery, and so tasty!

Here's What You Need

- 3 cups milk
- ½ cup semolina
- 1 teaspoon butter
- 1 tablespoon sugar
- ½ teaspoon salt

TOPPINGS:
Butter
Brown sugar

SAY WHAT?!

Semolina is a kind of coarse wheat flour that's often used to make pasta.

HERE'S WHAT YOU DO

1. Pour the milk into a medium pot. Turn the heat to medium-high and bring to a boil.

2. Slowly whisk the semolina into the hot milk. Keep whisking so it doesn't get clumpy.

3. Whisk for a few minutes until the porridge starts to thicken. Add the butter, sugar, and salt.

4. Remove the porridge from the heat. It will thicken more as it cools. Serve it warm in bowls.

5. Top the kasha with extra butter and a sprinkle of brown sugar.

6. Enjoy this yummy Russian breakfast cereal!

A WORLD OF EATS
Breakfast!

Kids across the globe eat lots of different things for breakfast. Try one of these for your first meal of the day tomorrow!

AUSTRALIA: toast and Vegemite

BRAZIL: roll, ham, and cheese

CHINA: steamed pork buns, rice, and soy sauce

FRANCE: baguette, butter, and jam

ICELAND: oatmeal porridge and cod liver oil

JAPAN: rice, miso soup, and pickled vegetables

MALAWI: porridge and potatoes

MEXICO: tortillas, eggs, and salsa

NETHERLANDS: bread and butter with chocolate shavings

TURKEY: cheese, tomatoes, spiced meats, and olives

UNITED STATES: cereal and milk

FRUITS
GLOBAL TASTE TEST

The world has so many amazing fruits in all shapes and sizes!

See how many you can find in your local grocery store, then give them a taste test.

PAPAYA

Cut off the skin, squeeze out the fruit, don't eat the seeds!

RAMBUTAN

BUDDHA'S HAND

"Kiwi" is also a nickname for someone from New Zealand.

KIWI

PERSIMMON

TAMARIND

FIGS

Figs are as old as dinosaurs! Fig trees grew around the Mediterranean Sea 100 million years ago.

PINEAPPLE

MANGO

Coconut palm trees grow in tropical areas around the globe.

COCONUT

DATES

The word "date" comes from *daktylos*, the Greek word for "finger."

SATSUMA ORANGE

CARAMBOLA

BLOOD ORANGE

Carambola (or star fruit) is native to Indonesia and the Philippines.

PITAYA

Pitaya is also known as "dragon fruit!"

POMEGRANATE

Pomegranate was a symbol of prosperity in ancient Egypt.

39

MEALIE MEAL
Bread

Makes 9 squares

In South Africa, some kids like to eat mealie meal, a porridge made of ground-up corn. For a taste of mealie meal, make this quick ground-corn (or cornmeal) bread.

Here's What You Need

- 1 cup cornmeal
- 1 cup flour
- ¼ cup sugar
- 1 tablespoon baking powder
- ½ teaspoon salt
- 1 egg
- 1 cup milk
- ¼ cup butter, melted

Preheat the oven to 375°F (190°C).

HERE'S WHAT YOU DO

1. Whisk together the cornmeal, flour, sugar, baking powder, and salt in a large mixing bowl.

2. In a separate bowl, whisk the egg. Then whisk in the milk and melted butter.

3.

Pour the egg mixture over the cornmeal mixture.

4.

Stir it all up.

5.

Butter the bottom and sides of an 8-inch square baking dish. Then scoop the batter into the dish.

6.

Bake for 25 minutes, or until the edges begin to brown. You'll know it's done if a toothpick inserted in the center comes out clean. Cool, then cut into 2-inch squares.

REAL KIDS COOK

Meet Zora (7), Xavier (10), and Maceo (7)

FAMILY HERITAGE:
Botswana, Norway, Russia, and South Africa

RECIPES WE'VE MADE:
Ginger ale (see page 66), latkes, and Christmas cookies

FAVORITE INTERNATIONAL FOODS:
Mexican (especially rice and beans and guacamole)

"We've made *magwinya*, deep-fried South African doughnuts!"

Wonderful WAFFLES

Makes about 5 waffles, depending on the size of your waffle iron

Wake up to a plate of steamy Belgian-style waffles! You'll need a waffle iron to make this recipe, so borrow one from a friend if you don't have one.

Here's What You Need

- 2 eggs
- 1⅔ cups milk
- ⅓ cup vegetable oil
- 2 cups flour
- 1 tablespoon baking powder
- 2 tablespoons sugar
- ½ teaspoon salt
- Cooking spray

OPTIONAL TOPPINGS:

- Strawberries
- Whipped cream
- Chocolate sauce

HERE'S WHAT YOU DO

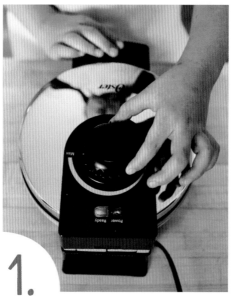

1. Set up a waffle iron on a table where you can easily reach it and turn it on.

2. Whisk the eggs in a large bowl until frothy. Stir in the milk and oil.

3.

In a separate bowl, whisk together the flour, baking powder, sugar, and salt.

4.

Add the dry ingredients to the milk mixture and stir until the lumps disappear.

5.

Spray the preheated waffle iron on both sides with cooking spray.

6.

Carefully pour about ½ cup of the batter onto the center of the iron. Close the lid.

7.

Bake until the waffle batter is cooked through, about 2 to 4 minutes. Most waffle irons will beep when the waffle is fully cooked.

8.

Repeat steps 5 through 7 until all the batter is used up. If you'd like, top the waffles with sliced strawberries, whipped cream, and/or chocolate sauce!

Coconut BREAD

Makes 1 loaf

Craving coconut?
Try mixing up this bread.
Slice it and serve it warm
with a little butter.

Here's What You Need

- 3 cups flour
- 1 tablespoon baking powder
- 1 teaspoon salt
- 2 eggs
- 1 (14-ounce) can coconut milk
- 1 cup grated coconut
- ½ cup sugar
- 1 teaspoon vanilla extract

Preheat the oven to 350°F (180°C).

HERE'S WHAT YOU DO

1. In a large bowl, whisk together the flour, baking powder, and salt.

2. In a medium bowl, whisk the eggs.

3.

Add the coconut milk, grated coconut, sugar, and vanilla to the eggs and mix well.

4.

Pour the coconut mixture over the flour mixture and stir it all up.

5.

Butter a loaf pan. Spoon the thick batter into the pan and smooth the top with a spoon.

6.

Bake for 1 hour, or until a toothpick inserted in the center comes out clean. Cool on a wire rack in the pan.

REAL KIDS COOK

Meet Malia (9) and Zadie (7)

FAMILY HERITAGE:
Belarus, the Kingdom of Tonga, Poland, and Sweden

RECIPES WE'VE MADE:
Potato latkes, chocolate chip cookies, and fresh lemonade

FAVORITE INTERNATIONAL FOODS:
Mexican and Japanese

"One year, we went to Tonga and helped roast a pig for Christmas dinner."

DRIKKE

Içecek

MERIENDA

NOSH

Đồ uống

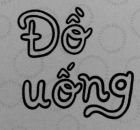

BANANA PUNCH, page 63

Chapter 3
⫸ SNACKS & DRINKS ⫷

Hungry for a snack? Nibble on toasted cashews from Costa Rica, sip a cool mango lassi from Nepal, mix up some hummus from Egypt, and quench your thirst with Liberian ginger ale, made with real ginger!

SPAIN
Pan con Tomate, 48

HUNGARY
Körözött, 50

NIGERIA
Plantain Chips, 52

EGYPT
Happy Hummus, 54

SYRIA
Pita Chips, 56

KOREA
Quick Kimchi, 60

COSTA RICA
Toasted Cashews, 62

JAMAICA
Banana Punch, 63

LIBERIA
Real Ginger Ale, 66

NEPAL
Mango Lassi, 68

GLOBAL TASTE TEST
Drinks, 64

PAN CON TOMATE

Makes 2 servings

Looking for a quick and delicious snack? Spanish kids smoosh a juicy tomato on a piece of toasted bread. They sometimes top the bread with cured ham, or *jamón serrano*, which you can find in the deli section of gourmet markets.

Here's What You Need

- 1 small baguette, hard roll, or round loaf of Portuguese bread
- 1 tomato
  Olive oil
  Salt
  Spanish ham (*jamón serrano*; optional)

SAY WHAT?!

Pan con tomate (pronounced PAHN kohn toh-MAH-tay) literally means "bread with tomato." **Jamón serrano** translates as "ham from the mountains" and is pronounced (k)hah-MOHN say-RAH-noh.

48

HERE'S WHAT YOU DO

1. Have a grown-up help you slice the bread carefully with a serrated knife. Toast the bread in a toaster oven.

2. Cut the tomato in half. Rub the pulp onto the bread, squeezing out the juices.

3. Drizzle a little oil over the tomato juice.

4. Sprinkle with salt. You can enjoy the tomato bread by itself or add a slice or two of ham.

A WORLD OF EATS
Piles of Paella!

Can you imagine sharing one dish of food with 110,000 people? The world's largest paella (*pah-AY-yuh*) — a Spanish casserole made with rice, saffron, fresh tomatoes, and lots of fish or chicken — fed that many people at a festival in Spain back in 2001. Most paellas are cooked in shallow, round, 12-inch pans. But the world's largest one was made in a pan that was 65 feet and 7 inches in diameter!

REAL KIDS COOK
Meet Kobi (7)

FAMILY HERITAGE:
Argentina, Germany, Hungary, and Ukraine

RECIPES I'VE MADE:
Körözött, challah, cupcakes, and banana bread

FAVORITE INTERNATIONAL FOODS:
Chinese and Italian

HUNGARY

KÖRÖZÖTT

Makes 2 cups (8 servings)

Many foods in Hungary are flavored with smoky paprika. Sample this spice on the tip of your finger. If you like it, you'll love this dip for bread and crackers!

Here's What You Need

- ¼ cup (½ stick) butter, softened
- 1 (8-ounce) package cream cheese, softened
- ½ small white onion
- 2 teaspoons ground smoked paprika
- 2 teaspoons caraway seeds
- ½ teaspoon salt

SAY WHAT?!

In Hungarian, this spread is pronounced *KUH-ruh-zuht.*

1. Unwrap the butter and cream cheese and place them in a bowl at room temperature.

2. Place the onion in a food processor and finely chop. Add it to the bowl of butter and cream cheese.

3. Add the paprika, caraway seeds, and salt to the bowl.

4. Stir until it's nice and smooth.

5. Spread the mixture on crackers or bread.

Yum!

Street Eats

All around the world, vendors cook and sell food right on the street. Here are a few street foods you might find in some countries.

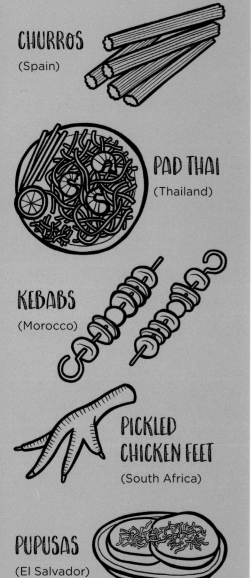

CHURROS
(Spain)

PAD THAI
(Thailand)

KEBABS
(Morocco)

PICKLED CHICKEN FEET
(South Africa)

PUPUSAS
(El Salvador)

NIGERIA

PLANTAIN CHIPS

Makes 4 servings

These crunchy, salty chips taste a little like potato chips. In Nigeria, street vendors deep-fry their chips in coconut oil. Here's a version that you can bake in the oven without the hot oil. You can find plantains in the grocery store near the bananas. They look similar, but plantains are bigger and greener than bananas.

Here's What You Need

- 2 green plantains
- 2 tablespoons coconut oil, melted (or olive oil)
- ¾ teaspoon salt

Preheat the oven to 400°F (200°C).

1. Cut off both ends of each plantain, then cut them in half.

2. Peel the plantains. Slice them into coins as thin as you can.

3. Mix the plantain slices, oil, and salt in a medium bowl. Stir to coat the plantain slices.

4. Lightly grease a baking sheet. Arrange a single layer of plantain slices on the baking sheet.

5. Bake for 20 minutes, turning once with tongs halfway through the cooking time.

6. Remove from the oven when the chips begin to brown on the edges. Serve warm.

Happy HUMMUS

Makes 6–8 servings

Skip the store-bought hummus and try making from scratch this tasty chickpea spread that's popular throughout the Middle East and beyond. Serve it with pita chips (see page 56) and cut-up veggies for a healthy snack.

Here's What You Need

- 1 (15-ounce) can chickpeas
- 1 garlic clove
- ½ teaspoon salt
- 3 tablespoons tahini paste
- 2 tablespoons lemon juice (about half a lemon)
- 1 tablespoon olive oil
  Toppings of your choice (optional)

SAY WHAT?!

Tahini is a smooth paste made from ground sesame seeds.

HERE'S WHAT YOU DO

1. Drain the canned chickpeas, saving the liquid in a measuring cup.

2. Peel the garlic clove and place it into a food processor. Process until it's finely minced.

3.

Add the chickpeas, salt, tahini, lemon juice, and oil to the food processor. Purée the mixture.

4.

Turn off the food processor and add 1 tablespoon of the reserved liquid from the chickpeas. Purée until the consistency is nice and creamy.

5.

You can add up to 2 more tablespoons of the chickpea liquid if you want your hummus extra creamy. The hummus will thicken in the fridge.

6.

Transfer the hummus to a bowl. If you'd like, sprinkle with any of the toppings listed at right, or drizzle with a little olive oil. Store in the refrigerator.

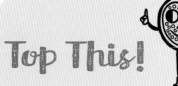

Top This!

Sprinkle a pinch of extra flavor on your hummus.

CUMIN

POMEGRANATE SEEDS

PINE NUTS

PAPRIKA

CHOPPED PARSLEY

55

PITA CHIPS

Makes 3–4 servings

These crispy snacks are a cinch to make — and they're the perfect scoop for Happy Hummus (page 54).

Here's What You Need

2 pita pocket breads
¼ cup olive oil
1 garlic clove, crushed
½ teaspoon salt

Preheat the oven broiler.

HERE'S WHAT YOU DO

1.

Cut open each pita pocket with kitchen scissors.

2.

Place the pitas, one at a time, on a cutting board. Using a pizza wheel, cut into eight triangles.

3.

Lightly oil a baking sheet. Arrange the triangles in a single layer on the baking sheet.

4.

Mix the oil, garlic, and salt in a shallow bowl.

5.

Using a pastry brush, paint the oil mixture evenly over the pita triangles.

6.

Broil the pita chips for a minute or two, until they are light brown and crispy. Watch closely because they burn fast!

Snacks around the World

Crunchy, salty snacks are popular around the globe. Here are some popular ones you may have never heard of before.

PLANTAIN CHIPS

(see page 52) from the Caribbean, Southeast Asia, and sub-Saharan Africa

NORI

(seaweed chips) from Japan

BISSLI (crunchy fried pasta)

from Israel

CHICHARRONES

(fried pork rinds) from Latin America and Spain

BILTONG (salted, dried meat)

from South Africa

POTATO CHIPS

(known as "crisps" in the UK) from the United States and the United Kingdom

Middle Eastern Meze

Throughout many Middle Eastern countries, people enjoy meze (pronounced MEH-zay), what we call appetizers. You can buy traditional mezes in your local grocery store — or make some of your own! Set up a buffet of the following items and invite your friends to serve themselves a little of each dish.

TZATZIKI

(a creamy yogurt dip from Greece)

BABA GHANOUSH

(an eggplant spread)

TERRIFIC TABBOULEH (page 78)

FALAFEL

HAPPY HOMMUS (page 54)

PITA BREAD

FETA CHEESE

OLIVES AND STUFFED GRAPE LEAVES

Hospitality is a virtue throughout the Middle East. When entertaining, hosts prepare enough food for their guests to have seconds, even thirds. And they always make their guests feel welcome. When you invite friends over for a meze party, be sure to use these Middle Eastern manners.

ENTERTAINMENT

Download and play some traditional Greek, Turkish, Persian, or Israeli music.

ATTIRE

Wear a burnoose, a traditional hooded cloak. To make your own, drape a long scarf or cloth over your head, then tie a cord or cotton belt around your forehead to hold it in place.

SAY WHAT?!

Meze foods not only are good to eat but have names that are fun to say! **Tzatziki** (pronounced [t]sad-ZEE-kee) rhymes with "weekly." Try saying **baba ghanoush** (bah-buh guh-NOOSH) three times fast!

Quick KIMCHI 🍴

Makes 4–6 servings

This spicy, tangy Korean condiment is perfect for noodles, rice, or dumplings. There are many ways to make kimchi, and most take a few weeks to ferment. Here's a quick version you can make in just a few hours. You can find *gochugaru* powder at international grocery stores.

Here's What You Need

- 1 small head napa cabbage
- 2 tablespoons salt

FLAVOR PASTE
- 1 tablespoon salt
- 1 tablespoon ground *gochugaru* pepper (Korean hot pepper)
- 3 tablespoons sugar
- 3 tablespoons rice wine vinegar
- 3 tablespoons toasted sesame oil
- 3 tablespoons toasted sesame seeds

SAY WHAT?!

Gochugaru (pronounced koh-CHOO-kah-roo) is made from sun-dried chile peppers.

HERE'S WHAT YOU DO

1. Have a grown-up help you cut the cabbage: First cut it in half lengthwise. Then cut each half into thirds. Cut the thirds into 1-inch pieces.

2. Place the cabbage in a large bowl. Sprinkle with the 2 tablespoons of salt. Stir it up and let sit for 30 to 60 minutes.

3.

Rinse and squeeze the cabbage. Drain out all the liquid from the bowl.

4.

Make the flavor paste by mixing the 1 tablespoon of salt, *gochugaru* pepper, sugar, vinegar, oil, and sesame seeds.

5.

Add the paste to the cabbage and stir it up well.

6.

Cover and refrigerate for at least 1 hour and up to 1 week. Use as a topping to liven up a noodle or rice dish.

REAL KIDS COOK
Meet Coco (9)

FAMILY HERITAGE:
Korea and Scotland

RECIPES I'VE MADE:
Kimchi and chocolate chip cookies

FAVORITE INTERNATIONAL FOODS:
Chinese

"My parents own a restaurant that's called Coco (named after me!)"

Toasted CASHEWS

Makes 1 cup

Have you ever seen a cashew tree? The nut dangles on the end of the fruit! If you're lucky enough to visit Costa Rica, you might see one there. For a quick snack and a taste of Costa Rica, roast up some cashews.

Here's What You Need

1 cup raw cashews
Salt

Preheat the oven or toaster oven broiler.

HERE'S WHAT YOU DO

1. Pour the cashews into a 9-inch square pan or into the tray of the toaster oven.

2. Broil the nuts for 2 to 5 minutes, or until they start to brown. Watch them closely! Cashews burn if they cook too long. Remove from the oven or toaster oven.

3. When the nuts have cooled, sprinkle with a little salt. Spoon into a bowl and enjoy!

BANANA Punch

Makes 4 servings

This refreshing smoothie will cool you off and fill you up on a hot day. Bananas grow in Jamaica and throughout the Caribbean, and this recipe is a great way to use up ripe ones. The riper the banana, the sweeter the shake!

Here's What You Need

- 2 ripe bananas
- 1 cup vanilla ice cream
- 3 cups milk
- ½ teaspoon vanilla extract
- ¼ teaspoon ground cinnamon
- ¼ teaspoon ground nutmeg

HERE'S WHAT YOU DO

1. Slice the bananas and put them in a blender.

2. Add the ice cream, milk, vanilla, cinnamon, and nutmeg.

3. Put the lid on the blender, then blend until smooth and creamy. Pour into glasses and enjoy!

DRINKS
GLOBAL TASTE TEST

Fill your glass with a global drink! Here are some favorites that kids around the world enjoy. You can order some of them at international restaurants. Others you can buy in your grocery store. Sip sip hooray!

UNITED STATES
RASPBERRY SMOOTHIE

LATIN AMERICA
ORANGE & LIME JARRITOS

THAILAND
TAMARIND NECTAR

THAILAND
STRAWBERRY FANTA

UNITED STATES
HOT APPLE CIDER

INDIA
CHAI
(a sweet and spicy tea made with milk)

MOROCCO
MINT TEA

CHINA
BOBA "BUBBLE" TEA
(sweet tea with tapioca)

TURKEY
CHERRY JUICE

64

GERMANY
PAULANER SPEZI
(orange cola)

CUBA & JAMAICA
MANGO BATIDO
(and other fruit smoothies)

SOUTH & SOUTHEAST ASIA
MANGO JUICE

NORTHERN EUROPE & UNITED STATES
MILK

BRAZIL
GUARANA SODA

GHANA
MALTA GOYA

THAILAND
TAMARIND NECTAR

NORTH AFRICA
ORANGINA

SINGAPORE
BLACK SOY MILK

ITALY
SAN PELLEGRINO BLOOD ORANGE

MEXICO
HOT CHOCOLATE

CHINA
GREEN TEA

65

Real
GINGER ALE

Makes about 4 cups of syrup and 16 cups of ginger ale

Are you a fan of ginger ale? Then try making the real thing. The main ingredient is fresh ginger, the root of a plant that grows across much of Africa. Keep a jar of this soda syrup in your refrigerator and mix yourself a refreshing glass of ginger ale to quench your thirst whenever you want.

Here's What You Need

1 pound fresh ginger
6 cups water
1 cup sugar
Ice cubes
Seltzer water
Lemon slice

1. Ask a grown-up to help you peel and dice the ginger. See page 19 to learn how.

2. Stir the ginger, water, and sugar together in a large saucepan. Bring to a boil, then reduce the heat to low. Simmer for 30 minutes, stirring occasionally.

3. Turn off the heat and let the mixture cool completely.

4. Set a strainer over a bowl or pitcher. Pour the liquid through the strainer to remove the ginger pieces. You now have ginger syrup.

5. To make the ginger ale, pour into a tall glass about ¼ cup of the syrup (or more if you want a stronger ginger flavor).

6. Add ice cubes and fill the glass with seltzer water. Stir with a tall spoon and serve topped with a lemon slice.

NEPAL

Mango LASSI

Makes 2–3 servings

Enjoy a Nepalese-style smoothie! Lassi yogurt drinks are cool and creamy — and popular throughout India and Nepal. Use fresh or frozen mango.

Here's What You Need

- 2 cups chopped frozen or fresh mango
- 1 cup plain yogurt
- ½ cup milk
- ¼ cup sugar (or less or more to taste)
  Ground cardamom (optional)

HERE'S WHAT YOU DO

1.
Place the mango, yogurt, milk, and sugar into a blender.

2.
Put on the lid and blend until nice and creamy, about a minute or two. Pour into tall glasses. Sprinkle each glass with a pinch of cardamom, if you'd like.

SHERPA POPCORN

Kids who live in the Himalayas, a Nepalese mountain range, grow and eat popcorn. They cook it over wood or coal fires in big black pots. Try this microwave version — and flavor it with a sprinkle of sugar like kids do in Nepal!

Makes 5 cups

HERE'S WHAT YOU NEED

3 tablespoons popcorn kernels
¼ teaspoon sugar

HERE'S WHAT YOU DO

1. Measure the popcorn kernels into a paper bag. Fold over the top of the bag twice. Microwave for 2 to 3 minutes, or until the popping almost stops.

2. Remove the bag from the microwave. Open the bag carefully to let the steam escape. Add the sugar, close the bag, and shake to mix.

3. Eat right away.

Chapter 4
LUNCH

Enjoy the flavors of some of the world's best midday meals, including Japanese ramen noodle soup, French croque monsieur sandwiches, and Greek salad. *Bon appétit!*

FRANCE
Croque Monsieur, 72

ITALY
Caprese Salad, 74

GREECE
Greek Salad, 76

ISRAEL
Terrific Tabbouleh, 78

VIETNAM
Banh Mi Sandwiches, 80

JAPAN
Ramen Noodle Soup, 82

PERU
Beef Empanadas, 84

AUSTRALIA
Sausage Rolls, 86

GLOBAL TASTE TEST:
Breads, 88

CROQUE MONSIEUR

Makes 2 sandwiches

These cooked ham-and-cheese sandwiches are a quick and filling lunch. They are traditionally made with a creamy white sauce called béchamel. Here's a simpler version that's a little closer to a French toast sandwich filled with ham and melted cheese.

Here's What You Need

- 4 slices white or sourdough bread
- 4 slices ham
- 4 slices Swiss or cheddar cheese
  Mustard (optional)
- 1 egg
- 3 tablespoons milk
  Pinch of salt
- ¾ tablespoon butter

SAY WHAT?!

In French, the phrase **croque monsieur** (pronounced krahk muh-SYUHR) literally translates as "(one) bites (the) gentleman with a crunch."

HERE'S WHAT YOU DO

1. Make two simple ham-and-cheese sandwiches, spreading one slice of bread for each sandwich with mustard, if you'd like.

2. Whisk the egg, milk, and salt in a shallow bowl.

3.

Melt the butter in a frying pan or an electric skillet over medium-high heat. Dip one side of one sandwich in the egg batter, then dip the other side and place in the hot pan.

4.

Dip both sides of the second sandwich in the egg batter and set it in the pan next to the first one. Cook the sandwiches on the first side until golden brown, about 3 minutes.

5.

Flip the sandwiches with a spatula. Cook on the second side for another 3 minutes.

6.

Using a spatula, move the sandwiches from the pan to a plate, slice them in half, and serve.

GET CREATIVE
Want Fries with That?

Serve French fries as a side dish. Here's what people around the world put on their fries.

CANADA & ENGLAND:
vinegar and salt

GERMANY & BELGIUM:
mayonnaise

UNITED STATES:
ketchup

CAPRESE
Salad

Makes 4 servings

This Italian antipasto (starter dish) is easy to make and delicious, especially if you use basil and tomatoes when they are in season. The salad features all the colors of the Italian flag: green, white, and red. Serve it with crusty Italian bread.

Here's What You Need

About 12 fresh basil leaves
2 large ripe tomatoes, sliced into rounds
½ pound fresh mozzarella, sliced into rounds
2–3 tablespoons olive oil
Salt and pepper

HERE'S WHAT YOU DO

1. Rinse the basil leaves and pat dry with a paper towel. Pinch off the stems.

2. Place a tomato slice on a plate. Overlap it with a slice of mozzarella and a basil leaf. Repeat until you have filled the plate.

3. Drizzle with the oil. Sprinkle with salt and pepper.

GET CREATIVE
Antipasti Platter

Entertaining friends and family? Serve up an Italian-style first course. Assemble a platter with any of the following Italian favorites. Enjoy!

Meats: prosciutto, salami, or coppa (Italian sausage)

Marinated vegetables: artichoke hearts, roasted red peppers, or *peperoncino* (chile pepper)

Cheeses: Parmesan, Asiago, provolone, or fontina, thinly sliced

Bread: breadsticks, ciabatta, or focaccia

Olives: kalamata or Niçoise

REAL KIDS COOK
Meet Leo (9)

FAMILY HERITAGE:
Greece and India

RECIPES I'VE MADE:
Sub sandwiches and Greek salad

FAVORITE INTERNATIONAL FOODS:
Greek and Italian (pizza!)

"I love to eat pastitsio, a Greek baked pasta dish."

GREECE

GREEK Salad

Makes 4–6 servings

Traditional Greek salad doesn't have lettuce — just feta cheese, tomatoes, and olives. This variation is a twist on the classic (which is popular at Greek restaurants in the United States). Mix the dressing and all the ingredients together for a fresh, tasty side dish! You can store leftover salad dressing in the fridge.

Here's What You Need

DRESSING
- ½ cup olive oil
- ¼ cup lemon juice (about 1 lemon)
- 1 garlic clove, crushed
- 1 teaspoon dried oregano
- ½ teaspoon salt
- ¼ teaspoon black pepper

SALAD
- 1 head romaine lettuce, chopped
- 1 large tomato, cut into wedges
- 1 small cucumber, cut into half rounds
- 1 small red onion, sliced
- ½ cup kalamata olives, pitted
- ½ cup crumbled feta cheese

DRESSING

1. Pour the oil into a glass jar with a tight-fitting lid.

2. Add the lemon juice, garlic, oregano, salt, and pepper.

3. Shake it up and set aside.

SALAD

4. Place the lettuce, tomato, cucumber, and onion in a large salad bowl.

5. Top with the olives and crumbled feta cheese.

6. Drizzle the dressing over the salad. Toss with salad tongs.

SAY WHAT?!

Tabbouleh (pronounced tuh-BOO-luh) is popular throughout the Middle East, and each country's version is slightly different.

ISRAEL

Terrific TABBOULEH

Makes 4–6 servings

This traditional Middle Eastern salad is made of finely chopped parsley, tomatoes, and mint and a cracked wheat called bulgur. Serve it as a salad or spoon it into a pita pocket for a healthy sandwich.

Here's What You Need

- 1 cup bulgur (medium grind)
- 2 cups hot water
- ¼ cup lemon juice (about 1 lemon)
- ¼ cup olive oil
- 1 teaspoon salt
- 1 garlic clove, crushed (optional)
- 2 tomatoes, cored, seeded, and diced
- 1 cucumber, seeded and diced
- 1 cup peas (optional)
- 1 cup chickpeas (optional)
- 1 cup chopped fresh parsley (about 1 bunch)
- ½ cup chopped fresh mint

1. Put the bulgur into a large bowl. Pour in the hot water. Cover the bowl and let the bulgur sit until it is soft, about 45 minutes.

2. Place a strainer in the sink. Pour in the bulgur and water. Press to remove the liquid. Return the bulgur to the bowl.

3. Stir in the lemon juice, oil, salt, and garlic, if using.

4. Add the tomatoes and cucumber to the bowl. You can also add peas and/or chickpeas, if you'd like.

5. Add the parsley and mint. Stir up the tabbouleh. Give it a taste. Add extra salt, if you'd like.

6. Cover and refrigerate for at least 1 hour and up to 2 days.

REAL KIDS COOK
Meet Tao (5) and Song (8)

FAMILY HERITAGE:
England, Germany, Russia, and Vietnam

RECIPES WE'VE MADE:
Banh mi, pho, bao, summer rolls, cranberry relish, and pie

FAVORITE INTERNATIONAL FOODS:
Japanese and Korean

"We celebrate Tet [Vietnamese New Year] and the Autumn Moon Festival."

VIETNAM

BANH MI
Sandwiches

SAY WHAT?!
French colonists introduced Vietnam to the baguette, which helped create the **banh mi** (pronounced bahn mee) sandwich.

Makes 4 servings

Tired of your same old school lunch sandwich? Try this Vietnamese favorite made with pickled carrots and cucumbers, fresh mint and cilantro, and meat. The literal translation of *banh mi* is "bread," because the baguette is such an important part of this sandwich. Dig into one of the most delicious sandwiches in the world!

Here's What You Need

SANDWICH
- ½ cup white vinegar
- ½ cup sugar
- 1 cup shredded carrots
- 1 cucumber, sliced into strips lengthwise
- ½ cup fresh cilantro leaves
- ½ cup fresh mint leaves
- 1 baguette, sliced lengthwise
- 8 slices cooked ham, cooked chicken, or tofu

SPICY MAYONNAISE
- 3 tablespoons mayonnaise
- 1½ teaspoons sriracha hot sauce

1. Mix the vinegar and sugar in a medium bowl. Add the grated carrot and cucumber slices. This is an easy way to "pickle" raw veggies. Let them pickle for 1 to 6 hours, then drain off the liquid.

2. Chop the cilantro and mint and set aside.

3. Make the spicy mayonnaise: Mix the mayonnaise and sriracha sauce in a small bowl. Set aside.

4. Now you're ready to assemble the sandwich. Spread the spicy mayonnaise on the bread. Add a layer of ham, chicken, or tofu.

5. Top with the pickled carrots and cucumber slices. Sprinkle with the chopped cilantro and mint leaves.

6. Place the top half of the baguette on the sandwich. Slice into four portions for serving.

RAMEN NOODLE Soup

Makes 2 servings

In Japan, you can stop by a *ramen-ya* (pronounced RAH-mehn yah), or noodle shop, and get a bowl of soup for a quick, inexpensive, and filling meal. Make your own healthy, flavorful version with this recipe.

Here's What You Need

1	tablespoon sesame or vegetable oil
2–4	garlic cloves, crushed
1–2	tablespoons grated ginger
4	cups miso or chicken broth
2	cups water
1	tablespoon soy sauce
6–10	shiitake mushrooms, thinly sliced
1	carrot, cut into rounds
¾	cup diced firm tofu or cooked shrimp, beef, or chicken
2	(3-ounce) packages ramen or other Asian noodles
2	scallions, chopped

HERE'S WHAT YOU DO

1. Heat the oil in a medium soup pot over medium heat. Add the garlic and ginger, and cook for about 3 minutes.

2. Pour the broth and water into the pot. Add the soy sauce and turn up the heat to high.

3.

Add the mushrooms, carrot, and tofu, and cook for 5 minutes.

4.

Add the noodles and let the soup cook for about 3 minutes, or until the noodles are soft.

5.

Ladle the soup into bowls. Garnish with the scallions and any of the stir-ins listed below.

NORI

SESAME OIL

Extra Flavor

Stir any of these into your ramen noodle soup!

MIRIN (RICE WINE)

MISO PASTE

SESAME OIL

SOY SAUCE

HARD-BOILED EGG

NORI (SEAWEED)

BEAN SPROUTS

MISO PASTE

BEAN SPROUTS

PERU

Beef
EMPANADAS 🍴

Makes 10 empanadas

These tasty pocket pastries are popular in Peru. Add green olives and hard-boiled eggs to the spicy ground beef filling for extra flavor. You can buy empanada wrappers in the international freezer section of most grocery stores.

Here's What You Need

FILLING
- 1 tablespoon vegetable oil
- 1 small white onion, diced (about ½ cup)
- 2 teaspoons chili powder
- 1 teaspoon ground cumin
- 1 teaspoon garlic powder
- 1 teaspoon dried oregano
- ½ teaspoon salt
- 1 pound ground beef

EMPANADAS
- 10 empanada wrappers, defrosted if frozen
- 2 hard-boiled eggs, sliced (optional)
- ½ cup sliced green olives (optional)
- 1 egg (for the egg wash)

Preheat the oven to 375°F (190°C).

HERE'S WHAT YOU DO

FILLING

1.
Heat the oil in a skillet over medium heat. Add the onions. Sauté until the onions are soft, about 5 minutes. Then add the chili powder, cumin, garlic powder, oregano, and salt.

2.
Add the ground beef. Break up the meat into small pieces with the spatula. Stir and cook until the meat is brown, about 8 minutes. Turn off the heat and let the mixture cool.

3.

Place a defrosted empanada wrapper on a cutting board. Spoon into the center a tablespoon or two of the filling. Add a few slices of the hard-boiled egg and/or green olives, if you'd like.

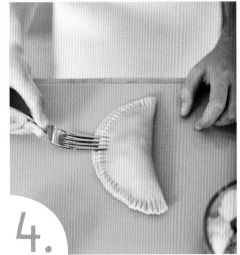

4.

Fold the round in half. Press the edges together gently with your fingers, then use a fork to seal the edges. Rub on a few drops of water if the edges dry out.

5.

Grease a baking sheet with vegetable oil. Transfer the empanada to the baking sheet. Whisk the egg in a small bowl. Brush the egg onto the empanada with a pastry brush.

6.

Repeat steps 3 through 5 with the remaining empanadas until you've used up all the filling. Bake for 20 minutes, or until golden on top.

Dipping Sauces

Serve your empanadas nice and warm with any of these dipping sauces.

TOMATO SAUCE

SALSA

CHIMICHURRI (page 93)

KETCHUP

Sausage ROLLS

Makes about 20 rolls

Looking for tasty finger food for a party? Try making these Australian party favorites. Dip the homemade rolls in ketchup or barbecue sauce.

Here's What You Need

1	pound ground sausage
1	teaspoon garlic powder
½	teaspoon salt
¼	teaspoon black pepper
1	teaspoon ground paprika
2	sheets (1 box) frozen puff pastry, defrosted
1	egg
1	tablespoon water

Preheat the oven to 400°F (200°C).

HERE'S WHAT YOU DO

1. In a large bowl, mix the ground sausage, garlic powder, salt, pepper, and ½ teaspoon of the paprika with a big spoon or clean hands.

2. Lightly flour a counter or cutting board. Use a rolling pin to roll out a defrosted puff pastry sheet into an 11- by 10-inch rectangle. Cut the rectangle into thirds with a pizza wheel or knife.

3.

Pat a long log of the sausage mixture down each of the three rectangles of pastry, as shown.

4.

Roll the pastry up over the sausage. Pinch the seams together. Repeat steps 2 through 4 with the second pastry sheet.

5.

Grease a baking sheet. Using a pizza wheel, cut each log into four pieces. Then place the pieces, seam side down, on the baking sheet.

6.

Whisk together the egg and water in a small bowl. Brush the mixture all over the pastry.

7.

Sprinkle with the remaining ½ teaspoon paprika.

8.

Bake for 20 to 25 minutes, or until the pastry is light brown and puffed up and the sausage is no longer pink.

BREADS
GLOBAL TASTE TEST

People around the world love to eat fresh-baked bread. It comes in many shapes and sizes, and it's made out of wheat, corn, or other kinds of flour. Visit international bakeries or restaurants and taste as many of these breads as you can!

(with hummus, page 54) PITA

MIDDLE EAST

UNITED STATES

SLICED WHITE BREAD

(with peanut butter)

GERMANY

PRETZEL (with mustard)

CHINA

BAO BUNS

INJERA **ETHIOPIA**

TORTILLA **LATIN AMERICA**

(with chutney)

NAAN **INDIA**

CROISSANT

(with jam)

ITALY
CIABATTA

FRANCE

Besseha

BUON APPETITO

¡BUEN PROVECHO!

AFIYET OLSUN!

ARROZ Y FRIJOLES NEGROS,
page 94

Chapter 5

⫸ DINNER ⫷

Turn the page and find out how to serve up dinner Ethiopian-style, cook up Indonesian chicken satay, and make a Lebanese staple of lentils and rice.

ARGENTINA
Cowboy Steak
with Chimichurri, 92

CUBA
Arroz y Frijoles Negros, 94

SWEDEN
Swedish Meatballs, 96

INDIA
Chicken Curry, 99

INDONESIA
Chicken Satay, 102

CHINA
Fried Rice, 104

LEBANON
Mujadara, 108

TURKEY
Lamb Köfte, 110

ETHIOPIA
Atakilt Wat, 112

MOROCCO
Shakshuka, 114

GLOBAL TASTE TEST:
Veggies, 106

COWBOY STEAK with Chimichurri

Makes 6 servings

Where in the world can you get the best steak? Beef experts say Argentina. To cook up their world-famous steaks, Argentineans host *asados*, or barbecues. They grill the beef over an open fire — the way people have been cooking steak for thousands of years. Serve your steak with the chimichurri sauce at right.

Here's What You Need

- 1 tablespoon olive or vegetable oil
- 2 pounds sirloin steak
  Salt

HERE'S WHAT YOU DO

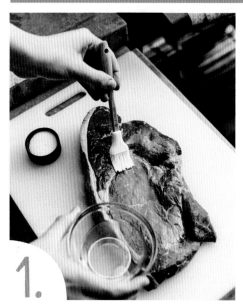

1.
Ask a grown-up to help you prepare the hot coals on a charcoal grill or light the flame on a gas grill. Brush the oil onto both sides of the steak with a pastry brush. Sprinkle both sides of the steak with salt.

2.
Grill the steak for 5 minutes. Flip the steak and grill for another 5 minutes. Make a slit into the middle of the steak to see if it is cooked to your liking. If it's too pink, cook it a little longer.

SAY WHAT?!

Asado (pronounced ah-SAH-doh) rhymes with avocado!

CHIMICHURRI SAUCE

In Argentina, chimichurri is a favorite condiment. It's a bright green, pesto-like sauce with a little tang made with fresh herbs, garlic, and vinegar. Use it on steak or potatoes or any other meats or vegetables for a taste of Argentina.

Makes 1 cup

HERE'S WHAT YOU NEED

- 2 garlic cloves
- 2 cups fresh parsley (leaves only)
- 2 teaspoons dried oregano
- 1 tablespoon white vinegar
- ½ teaspoon salt
- ¼ teaspoon red pepper flakes
- ½ cup olive oil

HERE'S WHAT YOU DO

1. Place the garlic in the bowl of a food processor and roughly chop.

2. Add the parsley, oregano, vinegar, salt, and red pepper flakes. Process until finely chopped. You may need to stop the motor and scrape down the sides of the bowl with a rubber spatula a few times.

3. Add the oil. Put on the lid and pulse a few times to combine. Scrape down the sides of the bowl.

4. Transfer the sauce to an airtight container and refrigerate for at least 2 hours and up to 1 week.

ARROZ Y FRIJOLES NEGROS 🥄🍴

Makes 4 servings

This simple dish is a staple in many Latin American countries. You can buy the key spice in the recipe — adobo — in the international section of most grocery stores.

Here's What You Need

- 1 tablespoon olive oil
- 1 small onion, diced
- 1 green bell pepper, diced
- 3 garlic cloves, crushed
- 1 teaspoon adobo
- 1 teaspoon sugar
- ½ teaspoon dried oregano
- 1 (15½-ounce) can black beans
- 1 cup white rice
  Lime wedges (optional)

HERE'S WHAT YOU DO

1. Heat the oil in a large pot over medium-low heat. Add the onion and pepper. Sauté until soft, about 5 minutes.

2. Stir in the garlic, adobo, sugar, and oregano.

3.

Pour the liquid from the beans can into a 2-cup measuring cup. Add enough water so the liquid measures 2 cups.

4.

Pour the liquid into the pot. Stir in the beans and rice.

5.

Turn up the heat and bring the rice and beans to a boil. Then reduce the heat to low. Simmer, covered, until the rice absorbs all the water, about 25 minutes.

6.

To serve, spoon onto a plate or shallow bowl. If you'd like, you can also serve with a squeeze of lime.

REAL KIDS COOK
Meet Matthew (6)

FAMILY HERITAGE:
Cuba

RECIPES I'VE MADE:
Tostones (fried plantains) and arroz con leche

FAVORITE INTERNATIONAL FOODS:
Cuban

> "My dad is from Cuba and I have lots of cousins in Miami."

SAY WHAT?!

Arroz y frijoles negros (pronounced ah-ROHS ee free-HOH-lays NAY-grohs) is an easy-to-make side dish.

SWEDEN

Swedish MEATBALLS

Makes about 40 meatballs

These tasty bites are popular at smorgasbords (see page 98), or potluck buffets, in Sweden.

Here's What You Need

½ cup breadcrumbs
¼ cup milk
1 pound ground beef
1 pound ground pork
1 egg, beaten
1 teaspoon salt
¼ teaspoon black pepper
¼ teaspoon ground allspice

¼ teaspoon ground nutmeg
Lingonberry jam (optional)
Creamy Sauce (page 98) and cooked noodles (optional)

Preheat the oven to 400°F (200°C).

1.

Mix the breadcrumbs and milk in a small bowl and let soak for a few minutes.

2.

Place the ground beef and pork into a large bowl. Add the egg, salt, pepper, allspice, and nutmeg.

3.

Add the soaked breadcrumbs. Mix all the ingredients with a large spoon (or clean hands).

4.

Shape the mixture into 1-inch meatballs and place the balls on an ungreased baking sheet.

5.

Bake for 15 minutes, or until cooked through and no longer pink in the middle.

6.

Serve them as appetizers speared on toothpicks with jam on the side. Or try them over noodles with the creamy sauce on the next page.

CREAMY SAUCE

Try this quick, tasty sauce for your meatballs!

HERE'S WHAT YOU NEED

- 1 cup beef stock
- 1 cup heavy cream
- 3 tablespoons flour
- 1 tablespoon soy sauce

HERE'S WHAT YOU DO

1.
Whisk all the ingredients in a large saucepan. Cook over low heat, stirring, until the sauce is creamy and thick, about 10 minutes.

2.
Add the meatballs to the pan and coat them in the sauce.

3.
Cook until the meatballs are hot. Serve over noodles.

SAY WHAT?!

Hushållsost (pronounced HOOS-hahls-OHST) means "household cheese" in Swedish.

GET CREATIVE

Throw a Smorgasbord!

A smorgasbord is a potluck party. Everyone who comes brings a favorite food and sets it on the table, buffet-style. Here are some things to serve at your Swedish-style smorgasbord:

- ⋆ Swedish meatballs
- ⋆ Sliced cucumbers with salad dressing

- ⋆ Sliced hard-boiled eggs
- ⋆ Thinly sliced smoked salmon with small rye bread squares
- ⋆ Swedish cheeses such as Hushållsost
- ⋆ Crisp crackers
- ⋆ Cold meats

- ⋆ Cherry tomatoes filled with cream cheese and topped with crumbled bacon
- ⋆ Pickled herring (try it, you might like it!)

Chicken CURRY

Makes 4 servings

Curry powder is the secret to this flavorful chicken dish. Many spices are in curry powder — cardamom, turmeric, cumin, coriander, cloves, and more. You can buy lots of different kinds of premade curry powder at the grocery store.

Here's What You Need

- 1 tablespoon vegetable oil
- 1 small onion, chopped
- 1 clove garlic, crushed
- 1 tablespoon curry powder
- ½ teaspoon salt
- 1 whole boneless, skinless chicken breast, cut into 2-inch chunks
- 1 cup coconut milk
  Hot cooked rice

Wash Up

Ever forget to wash your hands before you eat? In India, it's tough to forget because there are sinks right next to the dinner table. Kids wash their hands before they eat — and again after they eat. Why? Because they eat with their hands, and their hands can get pretty messy — especially when chicken curry is for dinner!

HERE'S WHAT YOU DO

1. Heat the oil in a large skillet over medium-high heat. Add the onion and garlic and sauté for 5 minutes.

2. Stir in the curry powder and salt.

continued on the next page

REAL KIDS COOK

Meet Dhyuthi (7) and Pranav (11)

FAMILY HERITAGE:
India

RECIPES WE'VE MADE:
Chapati, dosa, roti, and pani puri

FAVORITE INTERNATIONAL FOODS:
Indian, Mexican, and Italian

"Our family celebrates the Hindu festivals of Diwali and Holi."

CHICKEN CURRY, *continued*

3. Add the chicken and sauté until the outside is golden brown, about 5 minutes.

4. Pour the coconut milk over the chicken.

5. Bring the coconut milk to a boil, then reduce the heat to low. Simmer, uncovered, stirring occasionally, until the chicken is cooked through, about 10 minutes. Serve over cooked rice.

A WORLD OF EATS
India Night

In India, the foods and condiments are often put out on the table at the same time. Everyone serves himself or herself a little from each dish. They eat with their right hands, scooping up their food with chapati (round flatbread). Put out the following foods and serve them up Indian-style!

Chicken curry: See recipe on page 99.

Basmati rice: You can buy basmati rice in the grocery store or in a health food store. Follow the cooking directions on the package.

Chapati or naan: You can buy these breads in the frozen food section of some grocery stores. Warm them up following the package directions.

Condiments: Set out little bowls filled with golden raisins, chopped peanuts or cashews, grated coconut, plain yogurt, and chutney. Let everyone top their curry with the condiments they like.

Chicken SATAY

Makes 4 servings

This skewered chicken dish, grilled with a peanut-coconut sauce, is a favorite street food throughout Southeast Asia. Serve it with extra peanut sauce for dipping.

Here's What You Need

- 2 pounds boneless, skinless chicken thighs, cut into 1-inch chunks
- ½ cup peanut butter
- 1 cup coconut milk
- 1 tablespoon soy sauce
- 1 tablespoon lime juice
- 1 teaspoon mild curry powder
- 1 garlic clove, crushed
  Hot cooked rice (optional)

OPTIONAL TOPPINGS:
Cucumber strips
Crushed peanuts
Lime quarters
Chopped cilantro

Preheat the oven broiler or a grill.

Broil

SAY WHAT?!

Satay is just a fancy word for seasoned meat grilled on a skewer.

102

1. Thread the meat onto metal skewers and set on a tray or plate. Wash your cutting board and your hands well.

2. Combine the peanut butter, coconut milk, soy sauce, lime juice, curry powder, and garlic in a saucepan.

3. Cook over medium-low heat, whisking until creamy and thick. Turn off the heat and let the mixture cool.

4. Spoon half of the cooled sauce over the chicken.

5. Broil or grill the skewers for 15 to 20 minutes, turning once, until they are evenly cooked and light brown on each side.

6. Warm the remaining sauce in the saucepan over low heat. Pour the sauce into a bowl and serve with the chicken skewers for dipping. You can also serve with rice, cucumber strips, crushed peanuts, lime quarters, and cilantro.

FRIED RICE

Makes 4 servings

If you have leftover rice from last night's dinner, turn it into tonight's side dish with this Chinese restaurant favorite. Make sure to use cold rice instead of warm rice so that the finished dish is not mushy.

Here's What You Need

- 2 tablespoons vegetable oil
- ½ teaspoon sesame oil
- 4 scallions, sliced
- 1 cup frozen peas
- 1 medium carrot, peeled and grated
- 1 tablespoon grated ginger
- 1 garlic clove, crushed
- 3 cups cooked and chilled white rice
- 3 large eggs
- 1½–2 tablespoons soy sauce

HERE'S WHAT YOU DO

1. Heat 1½ tablespoons of the vegetable oil and all of the sesame oil in a large wok or skillet over medium heat.

2. Slowly and carefully (to avoid being splattered by hot oil!) add the scallions, peas, carrot, ginger, and garlic. Sauté the vegetables for a minute, stirring constantly.

3.

Add the rice and heat for 2 to 3 minutes, stirring occasionally.

4.

Break the eggs into a small bowl. Beat them with a fork or small whisk.

5.

Push the rice to the edges of the pan and pour the remaining ½ tablespoon vegetable oil into the center. Add the eggs and stir until they are cooked and scrambled.

6.

Stir the eggs into the rice until everything is mixed up. Add the soy sauce and heat for another minute or two, stirring often. Serve and pass additional soy sauce.

A WORLD OF EATS

Happy Birthday!

In China, it's a custom to eat noodles on your birthday. Eating long noodles means you'll live a long life!

Some other traditional Chinese birthday foods are hard-boiled eggs and dumplings.

Whatever you eat to celebrate the birthday, though, make sure you do it on or before the special day. Wishing someone a belated birthday is bad luck.

VEGGIES
GLOBAL TASTE TEST

Some cultures are famous for using certain vegetables in their cooking.
See how many of these veggies you can find in your local grocery store — then use them in recipes from around the world!

CHAYOTE

Botanically, eggplants are considered berries! But we eat them like vegetables.

TOMATILLO

EGGPLANT

Tomatillos make tasty green salsa.

POTATOES

SWEET POTATO

CHINESE CABBAGE

Potatoes were first grown in the mountains of Peru and Bolivia.

UBE

PEPPERS

The inside of an ube yam is bright purple and used in many Filipino desserts.

OLIVES

RED CABBAGE

Beets are the main ingredient in Russian borscht soup.

BEETS

AVOCADO

ARTICHOKE

Mash up avocado to make guacamole.

CAULIFLOWER

Pumpkins grow on every continent except Antarctica.

PUMPKIN

YUCCA

PARSLEY

MUJADARA

Makes 4-6 servings

For comfort food that's inexpensive and packed with protein, cook up some of this lentil and rice pilaf. You can buy both the lentils and rice in the bulk dried food section of your grocery store.

CUCUMBER

Here's What You Need

- 1 cup dried lentils
- 4 cups chicken or vegetable broth
- 2 cups water
- 1 cup white rice
- 3 tablespoons olive oil
- 1 large onion, chopped
  Salt and pepper

OPTIONAL TOPPINGS:

Chopped parsley
Chopped tomato
Diced cucumber
Plain yogurt

YOGURT

SAUTÉED ONION

TOMATO

SAY WHAT?!

Mujadara (pronounced moo-ZHAHD-duh-rah) is a common Middle Eastern dish. In each country, people call it and make it a little differently. This version is popular in Lebanon.

1. Rinse the lentils in a strainer and pick out any stones. Transfer the lentils to a soup pot and pour in the broth and water. Cook over medium heat for 30 minutes.

2. Reduce the heat to low and stir in the rice.

3. Cover and cook until the water is absorbed, about 20 minutes. (If the rice and lentils are still crunchy but the liquid is all gone after 20 minutes, add another cup of water and cook for 10 more minutes.)

4. While the lentils and rice cook, pour the oil into a skillet and add the onion. Sauté over medium heat until soft, about 5 minutes.

5. Add salt and pepper to the hot lentils and rice, tasting as you go, until you like the flavor. Scoop the mixture into bowls. Top with the cooked onions.

6. Add any of the toppings you like, if desired.

REAL KIDS COOK
Meet Salim (8)

FAMILY HERITAGE:
Morocco

RECIPES I'VE MADE:
Soups, pancakes, waffles, muffins, Moroccan meatballs, and *zaalouk* (eggplant ratatouille)

FAVORITE INTERNATIONAL FOODS:
Greek and Middle Eastern

"I love parsley — just eating it by itself!"

SAY WHAT?!
Many Middle Eastern cultures have their own version of this dish. In Turkish, *köfte* is pronounced KUHF-tuh.

TURKEY

LAMB KÖFTE

Makes 6–8 servings

You only need a few simple ingredients to make these Turkish meatballs, but their flavor is delicious! If your family doesn't like ground lamb, replace it with the same amount of ground beef.

Here's What You Need

- 1 small yellow onion, finely chopped
- 1 pound ground lamb
- ⅓ cup chopped fresh parsley
- 2 teaspoons smoked paprika
- 1 teaspoon ground cumin
- 1 teaspoon salt
- ½ teaspoon black pepper
- 6–8 bamboo skewers, soaked in water
- Hot cooked couscous (optional)
- Plain yogurt (optional)

Preheat the oven broiler.

1.

Line a baking sheet with aluminum foil. Have a grown-up help you position an oven rack 6 inches away from the broiler heat.

2.

Combine the onion, lamb, parsley, paprika, cumin, salt, and pepper in a large bowl.

3.

Toss the ingredients with your (clean!) hands until evenly blended. Be careful not to overmix so it doesn't get too mushy.

4.

Scoop out enough of the lamb mixture to shape it into a 3-inch log around a skewer. Place the skewer on the foil-lined baking sheet.

5.

Continue making logs, spacing them ½ inch apart on the baking sheet.

6.

Broil the köfte for 5 minutes. Remove from the oven, flip with tongs, and broil for 5 minutes more. Serve hot with couscous and yogurt (for dipping), if you'd like.

ATAKILT WAT

Makes 4–6 servings

This cabbage, potato, and carrot dish is full of flavor. You'll need to buy berbere, a spice mix that gives this dish a taste of Ethiopia. You can find it at specialty food or international grocery stores.

In Amharic, Ethiopia's official language, **atakilt wat** (pronounced AT-uh-kilt WAHT) translates as "spicy vegetable stew."

SAY WHAT?!

Here's What You Need

- 3 tablespoons olive oil
- 2 garlic cloves, crushed
- 2 tablespoons freshly grated ginger
- 1 small onion, chopped
- 3 carrots, peeled and cut into rounds
- 2 teaspoons berbere seasoning
- 4 small potatoes, peeled and cubed
- ½ small head cabbage, sliced
- ¼ cup water
- 1 teaspoon salt

HERE'S WHAT YOU DO

1.
Heat 2 tablespoons of the oil over medium heat in a large skillet with a lid.

2.
Add the garlic, ginger, onion, and carrots. Cook, stirring occasionally, for about 5 minutes.

3. Sprinkle in the berbere. Stir for about a minute, letting the seasoning get nice and fragrant.

4. Stir in the potatoes, cabbage, water, and ½ teaspoon of the salt.

5. Cover the pan, reduce the heat to medium-low, and cook for about 30 minutes, stirring every 10 minutes or so, until the potatoes are tender. If the mixture dries out, add a little water.

6. Drizzle the vegetables with the remaining 1 tablespoon oil. Sprinkle with the remaining ½ teaspoon salt. Serve in shallow bowls.

REAL KIDS COOK
Meet Mekdes (11)

FAMILY HERITAGE:
Ethiopia

RECIPES I'VE MADE:
Atakilt wat, pumpkin pie, pancakes, and latkes

FAVORITE INTERNATIONAL FOODS:
Mexican (burritos)

"I made atakilt wat at my school's family cultural night and served it in a slow cooker."

MOROCCO

SHAKSHUKA

Makes 4 servings

One of the best things about this classic stew is that you can make and eat it any time of day — for breakfast, lunch, or dinner! Serve it with a loaf of hearty bread for sopping up the yummy tomato sauce.

Here's What You Need

- 3 tablespoons olive oil
- 1 small yellow onion, chopped
- 1 large red bell pepper, chopped
- 2 garlic cloves, crushed
- 2 teaspoons ground smoked paprika
- 1¼ teaspoons ground cumin
- 1 teaspoon salt
- ½ teaspoon black pepper
- 1 (28-ounce) can chopped tomatoes
- 4 eggs
- ¼ cup crumbled feta cheese
- ¼ cup chopped fresh parsley
  Bread, for serving

Preheat the oven to 375°F (190°C).

Shakshuka (pronounced shahk-SHOO-kuh) means "a mixture" in Arabic.

SAY WHAT?!

114

1.
Warm the oil in a large cast-iron or ovenproof skillet over medium heat. Add the onion and bell pepper, and cook until they begin to brown, about 5 minutes.

2.
Reduce the heat to medium-low. Continue to cook, stirring occasionally, until the onion and pepper are soft, about 3 minutes more.

3.
Stir in the garlic and cook for 1 minute. Add the paprika, cumin, salt, and black pepper, and cook until fragrant, about a minute.

4.
Add the tomatoes and cook, stirring occasionally, until the sauce has thickened, about 10 minutes. Remove from the heat.

5.
Make four small wells in the mixture and crack an egg into each. Place the pan in the preheated oven. Bake for about 10 minutes, until the egg whites are set (for a firm yolk, bake for 2 to 3 minutes longer).

6.
Remove from the oven carefully. Top the dish with the feta and parsley. Serve immediately, with bread.

Reka

DOCE

SWEET

TAMU

Enjoy

S'MORES, page 124

Chapter 6
DESSERT

Sample Anzac biscuits – an oatmeal cookie from New Zealand and Australia – bake Zimbabwean cookies with sweet potatoes, and try a favorite dessert of Thai kids: sticky rice!

ZIMBABWE
Sweet Potato Cookies, 118

MEXICO
Arroz con Leche, 120

BRAZIL
Brigadeiro, 122

UNITED STATES
S'mores, 124

SCOTLAND
Sweet Shortbread, 126

THAILAND
Sticky Rice with Mango, 128

NEW ZEALAND
Anzac Biscuits, 132

TAHITI
Tahitian Vanilla Cupcakes, 134

GLOBAL TASTE TEST:
Ice Cream, 130

ZIMBABWE

SWEET POTATO Cookies

Makes 2 dozen cookies

Yams are important to cuisines in many African countries. They are easy to grow, and when stored in a cool place, they last a long time. For a taste of yams, try these cake-like cookies made with sweet potatoes, which are more common in the United States than yams. They are bright orange, sweet, and delicious.

Here's What You Need

- 2 cups flour
- 1½ teaspoons baking powder
- 1 teaspoon ground cinnamon
- ½ teaspoon baking soda
- ¼ teaspoon salt
- ¾ cup (1½ sticks) butter, softened
- ½ cup sugar
- 1 egg
- 1 cup peeled and grated raw sweet potatoes or yams
- 1 tablespoon grated lemon peel

Preheat the oven to 350°F (180°C).

1.

Whisk together the flour, baking powder, cinnamon, baking soda, and salt in a medium bowl.

2.

In a separate large mixing bowl, cream the butter and sugar with an electric mixer. Blend in the egg. Then mix in the grated sweet potatoes and lemon peel.

3.

Add half of the flour mixture to the sweet potato mixture and combine slowly with the electric mixer. Then add the other half of the flour mixture and combine.

4.

Scoop the dough with a cookie scoop or tablespoon onto an ungreased baking sheet. Space the cookies at least ½ inch apart.

5.

Flatten with the bottom of a drinking glass. (If the glass sticks, dip it in warm water.)

6.

Bake for 8 minutes. Let sit on the baking sheet for a few minutes. Then remove the cookies from the sheet and cool on a rack.

After-School Avocado

When kids in Mexico need a quick snack after school, they reach for a creamy avocado. You can tell if an avocado is ripe by touching it; it should feel tender, but not too mushy.

1. Ask a grown-up to help you cut the avocado in half. Twist off the top half, then scoop out the big avocado seed.

2. Squeeze some lime juice onto each half. Sprinkle with a little salt. Then dig in with a spoon.

SAY WHAT?!

Arroz con leche is pronounced ah-ROHS kohn LAY-chay and means "rice with milk."

MEXICO

ARROZ CON LECHE

Makes 3 servings

This creamy rice pudding is a favorite sweet throughout Mexico and many other Latin American countries. Stir up the pudding over the stovetop and season with a little cinnamon.

Here's What You Need

- ½ cup long-grain white rice
- 1¼ cups water
- 1 stick cinnamon
- 1 egg
- 2 cups milk
- ½ cup sugar
- ½ teaspoon vanilla extract
- ½ cup raisins
- Ground cinnamon (optional)

1. Measure the rice into a large pot. Pour in the water, then add the cinnamon stick on top.

2. Bring the water to a boil over high heat. Then turn the heat to low, cover the pot, and cook until most of the water is absorbed, about 15 minutes.

3. Crack the egg into a medium bowl. Whisk it, then mix in the milk and sugar. Pour the liquid over the cooked rice. Remove the cinnamon stick from the pot.

4. Bring the rice pudding to a boil over high heat. Turn the heat to low and cook, stirring often to prevent sticking, until the pudding thickens, about 30 minutes.

5. Stir in the vanilla and the raisins.

6. Serve the pudding warm — or refrigerate it and eat it cold. Sprinkle some ground cinnamon on top, if you'd like.

BRIGADEIROS

Makes 2 dozen truffles

Ready to roll? Stir up these chocolaty fudge truffles, then roll them in shredded coconut, nuts, and other tasty toppings. They're a favorite *docinho* (pronounced DOH-see-noh), or candy, in Brazil.

SAY WHAT?!

Brigadeiros (pronounced bree-gah-DAY-roh in Portuguese) were first made in Brazil in 1940.

Here's What You Need

- 3 tablespoons butter
- 1 (14-ounce) can sweetened condensed milk
- ¼ cup cocoa powder
- 1 teaspoon vanilla extract

OPTIONAL TOPPINGS:

Chopped walnuts, pecans, or pistachios
Chocolate or rainbow sprinkles
Mini chocolate chips
Shredded coconut

HERE'S WHAT YOU DO

1. Melt the butter in a saucepan over medium-high heat. Add the sweetened condensed milk, cocoa powder, and vanilla. Whisk or stir until the mixture starts to bubble.

2. Turn the heat to low. Cook the chocolate mixture, stirring often, until it is thick and fudgy, about 5 to 10 minutes.

3.

Butter an 8-inch square pan. Pour the chocolate mixture into the pan. Cover and refrigerate until firm, about 2 to 3 hours (or overnight).

4.

To make each truffle, scoop out a small ball of chocolate with a teaspoon.

5.

Wet your hands with water, then roll the ball quickly in your hands.

6.

Coat the ball in any of the toppings at right (or any other topping you want to try). Place on a plate. Repeat steps 4 through 6 for the rest of the batter, rolling each ball in a topping.

GET CREATIVE
Toppings

RAINBOW SPRINKLES

CHOPPED PEANUTS

CHOPPED PISTACHIOS

SHREDDED COCONUT

MINI CHOCOLATE CHIPS

123

UNITED STATES

S'MORES

Makes 4 s'mores

For an all-American summer treat, melt some marshmallows and chocolate chips on top of a graham cracker in the toaster oven.

Here's What You Need

- 1 cup mini marshmallows
- 1 cup chocolate chips
- 4 graham crackers, broken in half

HERE'S WHAT YOU DO

1.

Place a handful of mini marshmallows and chocolate chips on four of the graham cracker squares.

2.

Set the graham cracker squares on a toaster oven tray.

124

3.

Toast until the marshmallows and chocolate chips melt. Watch them closely, since they can burn quickly!

4.

When the marshmallows are lightly toasted and the chocolate is gooey, they're done!

5.

Remove from the toaster oven and top each s'more with a second graham cracker. Enjoy!

CAMPFIRE S'MORES

Having a backyard campfire? Roast some marshmallows and make these gooey, sweet treats.

- 4 graham crackers
- 1 (1.5-ounce) milk chocolate bar
- 4 large marshmallows

Break each graham cracker in half (so you have eight squares). Break the chocolate bar into smaller pieces. Cover four of the graham cracker squares with chocolate pieces.

Place each marshmallow on a long stick or skewer. Toast each marshmallow over the fire, turning the stick until the outside of the marshmallow is light brown.

Lay each toasted marshmallow (still on its stick) on a graham cracker square with the chocolate. Cover with a plain graham cracker square. Pressing down firmly on the top cracker to hold the marshmallow in place, pull out the stick.

SCOTLAND

Sweet SHORTBREAD

Makes about 24 cookies

Shortbread is one of the most famous Scottish cookies. It's traditionally baked and eaten around Christmas and Hogmanay, the Scottish New Year.

Here's What You Need

- 1 cup (2 sticks) butter, softened
- ¾ cup sugar
- 2¼ cups flour
- ¼ teaspoon salt

Preheat the oven to 325°F (160°C).

HERE'S WHAT YOU DO

1. Cream the butter and sugar in a large bowl with an electric mixer or spoon.

2. Add the flour and salt. Mix carefully on low speed until the dough starts to come together.

3.

Butter a 13- by 9- by 2-inch pan. Press the crumbly dough into the pan. Flatten the surface with a spatula.

4.

Use a fork to prick rows of marks in the dough.

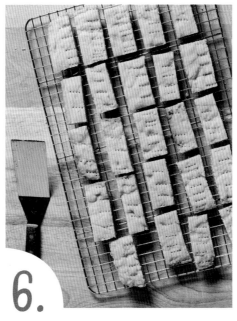

5.

Bake for 30 to 35 minutes, or until the edges begin to brown. Carefully cut the cookies into thin rectangles in the pan while they are still warm.

6.

Let the shortbread pieces cool for 15 minutes in the pan. Then transfer them to a wire rack to cool completely.

REAL KIDS COOK
Meet Olive (10) and Margaret (8)

FAMILY HERITAGE:
England and Scotland

RECIPES WE'VE MADE:
Chili, pancakes, blueberry muffins, and chocolate cupcakes

FAVORITE INTERNATIONAL FOODS:
Mexican

"We love to order chocolate pot de crème, a French custard dessert, at our favorite restaurant."

STICKY RICE
with Mango

Makes 4 servings

Rice for breakfast. Rice for lunch. Rice for dinner. And rice for dessert! That's what some kids in Thailand eat every day. Try making this popular sweet and sticky rice dessert. You'll need a bamboo steamer, a wok, and sweet sticky rice (available at international grocery stores and *not* to be confused with Japanese sushi rice!).

Here's What You Need

- 1 cup sweet sticky rice
- 1 tablespoon vegetable oil
- 1 cup coconut milk
- ½ teaspoon salt
- ¼ cup sugar
- 2 mangoes, cut into small cubes, or cubed frozen mango
  Black sesame seeds (optional)

HERE'S WHAT YOU DO

1. Put the rice in a bowl. Cover with 2 cups of water and the oil. Soak for at least 8 hours or overnight.

2. Line a bamboo steamer with parchment paper or cheesecloth. Drain the rice and spread it on the parchment paper or cheesecloth. Put the top on the steamer.

3.

Fill the bottom of a wok with a couple of inches of water. Carefully set the bamboo steamer into the wok. Cover with the wok lid. Steam the rice for 20 to 25 minutes over high heat.

4.

Heat the coconut milk in a saucepan over low heat. Stir in the salt and sugar, mixing until dissolved.

5.

When the rice is cooked, place it into a large bowl. Pour half or more of the warm coconut milk mixture into the bowl and mix it with the rice. Stir until the rice absorbs the coconut milk and the mixture is nice and thick.

6.

Serve the rice with cubed mango and a small pitcher of the remaining coconut milk for drizzling on top. Sprinkle with black sesame seeds, if you'd like.

A WORLD OF EATS

The Story of Rice

Historians say that rice originally came from what's now southern China. Travelers from other parts of the world carried it to their homes from China.

Today, more than 400 million tons of rice are grown and eaten around the world. Most of it grows in — you guessed it — Asia.

Rice is planted in paddies, big fields that are flooded with water. In mountainous areas, farmers plant rice on terraced hills, where it's watered by rainfall. When rice plants are young, they're bright green. They turn golden brown when they're ready to harvest. The tips of the plants, called panicles, hold the kernels of rice that we eat.

ICE CREAM

GLOBAL TASTE TEST

Invite friends over for a global sundae party. Put the smoosh-ins and toppings into little bowls. Then dig in and make sundaes with flavors that are popular around the world!

GROUND CARDAMOM

PISTACHIO NUTS

Pistachios add some Middle Eastern crunch.

MANGO

CHOCOLATE

MANDARIN ORANGE CHUNKS

Coconut is a flavor that's popular around the world.

COCONUT

CRUSHED TOFFEE BARS

CHOCOLATE CHIPS

RASPBERRY GELATO

Gelato is a soft, extra-creamy kind of ice cream from Italy.

130

SPRINKLES

Sprinkles are called "hundreds and thousands" in Australia.

WHIPPED CREAM

VANILLA

MARASCHINO CHERRIES

GREEN TEA

SLICED KIWI

Butterscotch sauce is a Scottish favorite.

BUTTERSCOTCH SAUCE

CRUSHED BUTTER COOKIES

BLUEBERRIES

BANANA SLICES

GET CREATIVE

Kiwi in a Cup

What Americans call "kiwi" is known throughout the much of the rest of world as the "kiwifruit." It's one of New Zealand's top agricultural exports, and people from New Zealand are sometimes called "kiwis." They got the nickname from a bird that's native to the island.

For a taste of the South Pacific, try this quick snack: Carefully cut off the top of the kiwifruit. Place it in an egg cup, cut side up. Drizzle with a little honey, then dig in with a spoon.

NEW ZEALAND

ANZAC Biscuits

Makes about 3 dozen biscuits

These popular "bickies" (an Australian term for cookies) were named after the soldiers in the **A**ustralian and **N**ew **Z**ealand **A**rmy **C**orps during World War I.

Here's What You Need

⅔ cup shredded coconut	½ cup (1 stick) butter
1 cup rolled oats	2 tablespoons golden syrup (or molasses)
1 cup flour	1½ teaspoons baking soda
1 cup sugar	2 tablespoons water
Pinch of salt	

Preheat the oven to 350°F (180°C).

SAY WHAT?!

What Americans call *"cookie"* is known as a *"biscuit"* in the United Kingdom, Australia, and New Zealand.

1.

In a large bowl, mix the coconut, oats, flour, sugar, and salt.

2.

Combine the butter and golden syrup in a medium saucepan over medium heat. Stir until the butter melts.

3.

In a small bowl, stir the baking soda and water together until the soda dissolves. Stir that into the melted butter mixture, then pour it into the flour mixture.

4.

Mix well with a spatula or spoon. Line a baking sheet with parchment paper.

5.

Roll the dough into 1-inch balls and place them on the baking sheet a few inches apart. (If your hands get sticky, dip them in a bowl of water.) Flatten them with your fingers.

6.

Bake for 15 minutes, or until the cookies are light brown. Let the biscuits cool on the baking sheet.

Tahitian VANILLA CUPCAKES

Makes 24 cupcakes

Is vanilla your favorite flavor? If so, you'll love these sweet and buttery vanilla cupcakes. Some of the best vanilla in the world is grown in Tahiti. If you can, buy a Tahitian vanilla bean and make vanilla sugar (see page 136) to sprinkle on top.

Here's What You Need

- 1 cup (2 sticks) butter, softened
- 2 cups sugar
- 4 large eggs
- 1 tablespoon vanilla extract
- 3 cups flour
- 1 tablespoon baking powder
- ¼ teaspoon salt
- 1⅓–1½ cups buttermilk

FROSTING
- 1 cup butter, softened
- 3 cups confectioners' sugar
- 1–2 tablespoons milk
- 1 teaspoon vanilla extract
- Vanilla sugar (optional)

Preheat the oven to 350°F (180°C).

1. In a large bowl, use an electric mixer to cream the butter and sugar until light and fluffy, about 5 minutes.

2. Beat in the eggs, one at a time, until combined. Beat in the vanilla.

3. In a separate bowl, whisk together the flour, baking powder, and salt. With the mixer on low, add half of the flour mixture to the butter mixture, beating to combine.

4. Beat in half of the buttermilk, then the other half of the flour mixture, then the rest of the buttermilk, mixing until just combined. Scrape down the bowl as needed.

5. Line two cupcake tins with paper liners. Scoop the batter into the cupcake tins until each cup is almost full.

6. Bake for 20 minutes, or until a toothpick inserted in the center comes out clean.

continued on the next page

GET CREATIVE

Top It Off with Vanilla Sugar!

Put about 2 cups of granulated sugar into a sealable container with a lid. Slice a vanilla bean in half the long way and scrape out the sticky black seeds. Bury the seeds and pod halves in the sugar. Cover the jar and let it sit for at least a week. Remove the pods and seeds and sprinkle the sugar on your cupcakes or on toast, or stir it into tea or warm milk!

7. Make the frosting: In a large bowl, blend the butter with an electric mixer (or mix by hand with a spoon).

8. Add the confectioners' sugar, 1 cup at a time. Stir in the milk and vanilla extract.

9. Spread the frosting on the cooled cupcakes with a butter knife. Or, to make your cupcakes a little fancier, put some frosting into a pastry bag and swirl frosting on top of each cupcake. Sprinkle with vanilla sugar, if you'd like.

INDEX

Download Some
FUN EXTRAS
for Global Feasts!

www.storey.com/global-feast-extras/

FLASH CARDS

How do you say "I'm hungry" around the globe? Download, print, and cut out these flash cards and quiz your friends!

I'M HUNGRY

in ARABIC

Anaa jaw'aan

(AN-uh zhuh-WAHN)

FOOD PASSPORT

Travel the world by tasting different foods! Download this food passport, print it, and fold it along the dotted lines. Then fill out your personal information on the first page. Add a check mark whenever you've tried a new recipe or dish from that place.

STOCK UP ON HOMEMADE FUN
with More Books from Storey

BY EMMA BIGGS, WITH STEPHEN BIGGS
With tips for how to grow a flower stand garden, suggestions for veggies from tiny to colossal, and ways to make play spaces among the plants, 13-year-old Emma Biggs offers original, practical, and entertaining gardening advice and inspiration.

BY RICKI CARROLL & SARAH CARROLL
Step-by-step directions teach how to make 10 cheeses kids love, including mozzarella, cream cheese, and feta. Easy recipes and lively serving suggestions will help you use your handmade creations in dips, spreads, sandwiches, and sweets.

BY AMIE PETRONIS PLUMLEY & ANDRIA LISLE
From sewing by hand to working on a machine, making a T-shirt quilt to adding pockets or darts, the best-selling Sewing School® series offers friendly instructions and step-by-step photography to guide young sewists in stitching up plenty of playful and practical kid-approved projects.

BY MARGARET LARSON
Learn key skills like how to drive a nail and operate a power drill. Then use what you've learned to build 17 fun and creative projects including your very own workbench, a clever portable tic-tac-toe game, a message board, and more.

JOIN THE CONVERSATION. Share your experience with this book, learn more about Storey Publishing's authors, and read original essays and book excerpts at storey.com. Look for our books wherever quality books are sold or call 800-441-5700.

Hear What Others Are Saying about the Best-Selling COOKING CLASS SERIES!

"Spiral-bound, with glossy, easy-to-clean covers, these cookbooks are bright and colorful, with recipes that range in difficulty from very easy (mug cake, salad dressing) to more complicated (crepes, spring rolls). They are perfect for children who want a thorough introduction to the kitchen, including basic rules for safety, vocabulary, setting a table and — you're going to love this, parents — cleaning up."

— *New York Times*

National Parenting Publications Awards Gold Winner

Parents' Choice Award Silver Winner

Mom's Choice Award Gold Winner

"Of all the kids' cooking books that have crossed my threshold over the years, this is the one that seems to have struck gold."

— T. Susan Chang, NPR

"A must-have for any budding chef. The recipe variations and open-ended projects let kids take their culinary creativity to the next level."

— *FamilyFun*

"No matter what you want to cook, this book has you covered, with helpful photos, easy-to-follow instructions, and quirky twists on recipes."

— *Foreword Reviews*

"When budding chefs see the photographs of creative food projects . . . they'll beg to take over in the kitchen."

— *Relish*

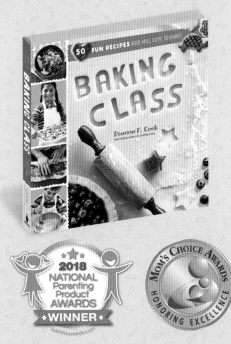

National Parenting Product Awards Winner

IACP Award Winner

Mom's Choice Award Gold Winner

"[A] teach-yourself-to-bake book with vast kid appeal, thanks to big step-by-step photos, clear instructions, and adorable, easy recipes (cranberry orange scones, teeny tiny apple pies, sugar cookies, macaroons). At the back are stickers, labels and — be still my beating heart — stencils so that you can sugar-powder your cookies into art."

— NPR

"What do we like more than homemade goodies? When kids can make 'em themselves! *Baking Class* helps them do just that with cute ideas and step-by-step how-tos perfect for any aspiring chef."

— FamilyFun

"A truly awesome cookbook for children of any age as soon as the child can reach the counter."

— Manhattan Book Review

"Roll up your sleeves and get out the oven mitts. This colorful, spiral-bound guide ... features easy instructions paired with helpful pictures. There are eye-catching recipes for crispy cheese squares (think Cheez-Its) and brownie pizza, plus adorable bread art (bake an octopus or a snail) and cake and cookie decorating ideas."

— BookPage

"Fifty easy-to-follow recipes with step-by-step photos that teach bakers-in-training to follow directions, measure ingredients, knead dough, make biscuits, decorate cookies, and produce a perfect pie."

— LA Parent

The mission of Storey Publishing is to serve our customers by
publishing practical information that encourages
personal independence in harmony with the environment.

Edited by Michal Lumsden

Art direction and book design by Jessica Armstrong

Text production by Liseann Karandisecky, Jennifer Jepson Smith, Erin Dawson,
and Kristy MacWilliams

Indexed by Nancy D. Wood

Cover photography by © Carl Tremblay, except © ToprakBeyBetmen/iStockphoto.com,
front, hand

Interior photography by © Carl Tremblay, except Mars Vilaubi, 9, 17 bottom left, 27, 47, 71,
91, 117, 133 bottom right and © Julie Bidwell, 24

Food styling by Joy Howard

Cover and interior illustrations by © Emily Balsley, except © Dima11286/Dreamstime.com, 7

Storey Publishing
210 MASS MoCA Way
North Adams, MA 01247
storey.com

Printed in Malaysia by DNP America, LLC
10 9 8 7 6 5 4 3 2 1

Library of Congress Cataloging-in-Publication Data on file

Storey books are available at special discounts when purchased in bulk for premiums and
sales promotions as well as for fund-raising or educational use. Special editions or book
excerpts can also be created to specification. For details, please call 800-827-8673, or send
an email to sales@storey.com.